FROM STATE CHURCH TO PLURALISM

FROM STATE CHURCH TO PLURALISM:

A Protestant Interpretation
of Religion in American History

FRANKLIN HAMLIN LITTELL

AldineTransaction
A Division of Transaction Publishers
New Brunswick (U.S.A.) and London (U.K.)

First paperback printing 2007
Copyright © 1962 by Franklin Hamlin Littell.

This book is printed on acid-free paper that meets the American National Standard for Permanence of Paper for Printed Library Materials.

Library of Congress Catalog Number: 2007020575
ISBN: 978-0-202-30921-7
Printed in the United States of America

Library of Congress Cataloging-in-Publication Data

Littell, Franklin H. (Franklin Hamlin), 1917-
    From state church to pluralism : a Protestant interpretation of religion in American history / Franklin Hamlin Littell.
       p. cm.
    Includes bibliographical references and index.
    ISBN 978-0-202-30921-7
    1. United States—Church history. 2. United States—Religion.
    3. Christian sects—United States. I. Title.

BR515.L55   2007
277.3—dc22   2007020575

TABLE OF CONTENTS

INTRODUCTION

The major problem before the churches in America is the achievement of self-understanding—more properly, the regaining of a consciousness of calling. A review of present thinking on the church, both theological and practical, shows a maximum of confusion in the pulpits and congregations. In some, there is still an effort to maintain standards of membership. In many, perhaps most, the infatuation with statistical success has led to the abandonment of Christian discipline. In Lent 1960, in Atlanta, Georgia, 462 individuals were admitted to a church on a single Sunday morning en bloc—without preparatory training and certainly without the baptism of repentance. In Nashville, Tennessee, in August 1960, young Christians, Negroes, were turned away from the doors of four churches by police —representatives of the civil government. No pastors objected. In Dallas, Texas, in the fall of 1960, a committee of churchmen announced they were opening a new Christian college to foster Bible study and "the American way of life." The remarks of an American theologian seem justified:

> . . . the Protestant church has confused its evangelical mission with organizational success.
> . . . ministers have learned nice people don't like ugly sermons.
> . . . underneath the enormous prosperity of the American churches there is a growing misgiving, shared by its clergy and laity, about the moral stamina of this nominal Christianity.[1]

The American churches seem well on their way to settling

[1] Waldo Beach, "Flip-Top Pulpits for Filter-Tip Faith," in *The News and Observer* (Raleigh, N.C.; July 26, 1959), Section III, p. 1.

for the status of culture-religion, scuttling the discipline and mobility which was once their pride.

Our conclusion might be that the American churches, once faithful and disciplined, have in their prosperity settled back into the world. And America, once a Christian nation, would seem well on the way to secularization and faithlessness. And in a certain sense this is right, for the standards of membership were higher when only 10 per cent of the population held church membership. The extraordinary growth of voluntary participation and support, during a century and a half of mass evangelism, was bought at the price of a steady depreciation of the theological, moral, ethical, and institutional discipline of the churches. But the idea that the American people were once Christian and have subsequently declined is false, and the historical perspective involved is unsound. America has never been a Christian nation except in the nominal sense. In the colonial period, state churches were maintained at public expense, as was the case in the home countries of Europe. But here too the establishments varied from the persecuting to the latitudinarian types, and true religion was uncommon in both cases. Those groups which today claim to look back to a lost virtue are as reactionary in church view as they usually are in economics. The time of the founding fathers was not an age of Christian virtue, "free enterprise," and "states' rights." Nor did America fall with F.D.R. and the New Deal, although the Protestant underworld and nativist groups generally are wont to formulate the issue in this way. The course of American church history has been marked, by and large, by the effort to win a people back to the churches they had frankly abandoned when support ceased to be compulsory, to Christianize and civilize an illiterate and semibarbarous people.

Most American church members are first-generation, or at best second-generation Christians. The problems which obtain, and they are many, are parallel to those which are found in all periods and places in church history where large masses of new converts affiliate with a religion whose implications they but vaguely grasp. Only once before in church history, when masses of Germanic tribesmen embraced the official religion of the Roman Empire, have such serious problems of education confronted the church. In the eighth, ninth, and tenth centuries the problems were polygamy, blood vendettas, brutal treatment of prisoners of war, the practice of religion as a tribal cult. In twentieth-century America, with over 60 per cent of the population affiliated and over 40 per cent attending, the problems are parallel: promiscuity and depreciation of the integrity and authority of the family, materialistic standards of success, racialism (the practice of religion as a tribal cult), widespread theological illiteracy. These are the problems of "Younger Churches," not of a Christendom in which the faith is reduced to a "post-Constantinian" status.

We come to the first major question in the churches' understanding of their role in the American setting: Is American Christianity to be interpreted as a part, and not too important at that, of European Christendom? Or are we in fact "Younger Churches"—with the problems characteristic of new Christians? For most of our history our religious life has been dominated by a view of church history in which the colonies and states were but deposits of European religious life. Until very recently American church history has been neglected by our seminaries. Except for the necessary attention to denominational chronicles, both church history and doctrine have been lined out as a continuum from the sixteenth-century Reformers to the present day. As a result, doctrinal issues have become more and more unreal—unrelated to the actual facts of the American scene.

For example, consider how unsatisfactory the terms "church," "sect," "denomination," "religious society," "religious association" have become. The terms are patently pejorative or inaccurate. For centuries of European Christendom, "church" was defined by law. Even Ernst Troeltsch, whose "church" and "sect" typologies have become a commonplace in American writing, identified "church" with that religious institution enjoying legal privileges; "sect" was a term applied to those outside the circle of privilege. But such use of the terms, however illuminating sociologically, is theologically senseless. A use of the term "church" which applied only to the legally privileged can mean nothing to the American setting and excludes the Early Church and "Younger Churches" as well.

In Christendom the ghetto was a political as well as religious entity. The relation with the Jews was thus defined in static fashion, relieved only by intermittent cruelty and insensitive Hebrew Missions. Following the horrors of the Thirty Years' War, relations between Protestant and Catholic state churches were defined geographically: the Peace of Westphalia (1648) allowed Lutheran, Reformed, and Roman Catholic adherents to emigrate to a friendly land without losing their lives. All other groups were relegated to the scorned status of "sects"; for generations they faced the death penalty for nonconformity—alternately condemned for "heresy" and "treason." But few Americans today are so religiously sociocentric as to term other religious groups "sects," and Jewish citizens are accorded full liberty of worship and cultic practice. Where then is "church," and what is a "sect"? Obviously, the terms which have been used so long in European lands with established "churches" are no longer applicable. The situation here is much more like that in other areas where religious affiliation is strictly voluntary—such as among the "Younger Churches."

For in America, although there is still social prejudice between groups which cling to the old cultural patterns, voluntaryism is the principle of our religious association. Sammy Davis, Jr., an American Negro searching for life's foundations, can become a practicing Jew by conviction. Arthur Cohen, born a Semite, can write of his religious choice:

> I have decided to embrace Judaism. I have not done so out of loyalty to the Jewish people or the Jewish state. My choice was religious. I chose to believe in the God of Abraham, Isaac, and Jacob; to acknowledge the law of Moses as the Word of God; to accept the people of Israel as the holy instrument of divine fulfill-

ment; to await the coming of the Messiah and the redemption of history.[2]

The late Roman Catholic bishop of Salt Lake was raised in
a fine Methodist family, and chose as an adult the faith and
career which he served with distinction. The present Protestant Episcopal bishop of California grew up a Catholic and
consciously chose the Episcopal church and ministry. An
American can choose, without loss of legal rights or privileges, to join any religious body or none at all.

Such a situation is new in human history. For all of pre-
Christian history and most of church history religious practice has been shaped by tribal or political loyalty. The
ancient religions of the Near East were all functions of civili-
zations. Only the God of Israel created a people. During
most of Christian history in the West, the baptized peoples
reverted to the use of Christianity as tribal religion. The voluntary appeal of religion—Jewish, Catholic, or Protestant—
is a new thing in church history. How are the religious
communities to understand their situation and what is required of them in it? By continuing to use phrases and
teachings which have nothing to do with it—by Jews' following the old regulations of the ghetto, by Catholics'
clinging to the views of Pope Leo XIII on Church and
State, by Protestants' quoting Luther and Calvin, or by facing openly and fearlessly the need to rework the terms of
reference and form of words so that there is some connection between fact and faith?

This is essentially our problem: to achieve a new self-
understanding, or consciousness of calling among the American churches. And in the process of denying an old pattern
of religious and political privilege, of accepting the implications of voluntaryism and pluralism, we must also achieve a
new understanding of the nature of the political covenant.
That men of different religious covenants may live together
as good fellow citizens is a fact—and also a profoundly important theological event. It means that the religious cove-

[2] Cohen, Arthur A., "Why I Chose to Be a Jew," 218 *Harper's
Magazine* (1959) 1307: 61–66, 67.

nants and the political covenants are separated. And that is the first phase of the genius of the American experiment— not "separation of church and state" (a misnomer, for we have *never* had it) but separation of the religious and political compacts. Our theoretical understanding has not, as yet, caught up with our experience.

This essay is an effort to understand and interpret how we arrived at our present situation. The writer is Protestant, but he writes with a profound appreciation for those Catholic and Jewish fellow citizens who are also attempting to find their way toward a definition of faithful obedience which is appropriate to the year 1961, in this good land we have been given for a heritage. In attempting to understand our situation, we are not ashamed to "discuss" with our fathers as well as our contemporaries. Nothing is more common than mere contemporaneity, except slavish adulation of the past. And in this dialogue with the past it is important that we listen as well as express our own opinions. The canon of the historical method requires, not that we be indifferent to the consequences, but that we give a fair hearing to all who have earned the right to be heard.

Two great church historians who have attempted to place the history of the church in America in its proper perspective, and instruct their students and coworshipers in the specific word which God had for these churches, were Philip Schaff (1819–93) and William Warren Sweet (1881–1959). Schaff, born and educated in Europe, never tired of emphasizing the importance of religious liberty to the enlivening of life and lay initiative in the American churches. That there were blessings to the civil society in the abandonment of coercion few doubted. But Schaff saw, a century before the seminaries ceased to apply Luther and Zwingli and Calvin untranslated and unmodified to church life in the New World, that a fundamentally different style of church life would inevitably develop. He viewed the prospect with enthusiasm and strove mightily to overcome the one great danger he saw in unrestrained religious liberty: the possibility that the freedom of the churches would be wasted and dissipated in unprofitable sectarian controversy.

To encourage co-operation between the churches Professor Schaff served for decades as American secretary of the Evangelical Alliance, carrying this along with his extraordinary service with the committee for the American Revised Version, his publication of the Schaff-Herzog *Encyclopedia,* his *Creeds of Christendom* (three massive volumes), his *History of the Christian Church* (six large volumes), etc. Like those who in earlier years came to the New World covenanting together to walk "in all his ways made known or *to be made known*" (italics mine), Schaff had tremendous confidence in the future of Christianity in America.

> The Reformation of the 16th Century is by no means the last word which God has spoken to His people. He has other and greater Pentecosts in store. By His providence all nationalities and creeds are brought together in this land of freedom, of which the reformers could not dream. Here is the material, the possibility and opportunity for a settlement of the controversies of Christendom. . . . If Christians are ever to be united, they must be united in Christ, their living head and the source of their spiritual life.[3]

Again, he wrote of his expectation of future flowering of Christian thought in his adopted land:

> America will no doubt produce, in due time, a classical theology of its own, that shall rise superior to the sectional and denominational schools, which so far have mostly prevailed amongst us, and be truly catholic in spirit, and influence.[4]

Is the time approaching of which Schaff prophesied? There are some indications that it is, that denominational differ-

[3] Quoted in Schaff, David H., *The Life of Philip Schaff* (New York: Charles Scribner's Sons, 1897), pp. 472–73.

[4] Schaff, Philip, *Germany; Its Universities, Theology, and Religion . . .* (Philadelphia and New York: Lindsay and Blakiston/Sheldon, Blakeman and Co., 1857), p. 8.

ences are making less significance as the community of ecumenical thought and action grows. At the same time, there are indications that Protestant nativism is far from dead: indeed, the flood of reactionary literature which identifies Christianity with a certain type of political and economic thinking continues to swell, and during the 1960 presidential campaign there was a nasty upsurge—happily fruitless—of the same bigotry and blind prejudice that disgraced the republic in 1928.

William Warren Sweet was in his generation the outstanding interpreter of American church history, and he carried the argument two steps further. He applied his attention to the role of the frontier in shaping American religion with great industry and success. His monographs and source books on the westward movement of the churches and the civilizing effect of the churches upon a semiliterate and half-barbarous people are extremely valuable. Moreover, he perceived that Christianity in America reflected more fully the "left wing" of the Reformation than it did the attitudes and practices of the state-church Reformations.

> The one fact, more than any other, which explains American religion in the period of the colonies is that the colonial churches were largely planted by religious radicals. With hardly an exception, the leaders in the establishment of the American colonies were liberal and even radical in both their religious and political views.[5]

It remained, however, for Kenneth Scott Latourette, historian of the expansion of Christianity, to begin to put the American situation in its proper perspective beside other times and places of extraordinary energy and growth.

> As the history of Christianity is usually written and taught, the impression is all too often given that the climax was reached with the Protestant and Catholic reformations and that everything which has happened

[5] Sweet, William Warren, *The Story of Religion in America* (New York and London: Harper & Bros., 1939), p. 2. 1st edition.

since has been in the nature of a postlude. It is as though the Christian drama had come to an end with the Reformation and that subsequent events have been akin to curtain calls. Both the scholar and the reader are led to the conclusion that in the last four centuries Christianity has been a waning force. . . .

The fashion in which millions of Christians have voluntarily contributed financially to the propagation of their faith at home and abroad has in magnitude been without precedent in the history of Christianity or of any other religion or set of ideas.[6]

Professor Latourette has also emphasized the importance of the Free Churches, which have carried the chief weight of foreign missions for many decades.

It is a contemporary German scholar, Professor Ernst Benz of Marburg, who has done the most to point out the significance of Dr. Latourette's studies for the interpretation of church history as a whole. In a recent volume, *Kirchengeschichte in Ökumenischer Sicht*,[7] he has published an intensive discussion of the Latourette style of universal history and gone on to contrast the expanding horizons of the Free Churches with the provincialism of most European historiography. And indeed the perspectives are most peculiar in many of the basic manuals in use in the European theological faculties. A representative example would be the *Kompendium der Kirchengeschichte* prepared by Professor Karl Heussi, which has gone through nearly a dozen editions over fifty years. This manual outlines the way in which the German nation inherited the custodianship of Christianity from the Holy Roman Empire and the Mediterranean matrix which preceded it; at the end the author tosses in three pages on "Christianity outside Germany"![8]

Even more astonishing than finding this provincialism in

[6] Latourette, Kenneth Scott, "New Perspectives in Church History," XXI *The Journal of Religion* (1941) 4:432–43, 438, 442.

[7] Published by E. J. Brill, Leiden & Köln, 1961.

[8] Published by J. C. B. Mohr, Tübingen, 1949 (10th revised edition here noted).

contemporary European writers is the fact that manuals treating the American development as a footnote to European Christendom are still commonly used in American seminaries. Whereas general history departments have long since moved on to study and interpret the uniqueness of the American situation, American church history is still a neglected study in most American seminaries and schools of religion. With the conservatism so common in religious circles, church history in its American manifestation is still taught largely as a relatively unimportant extension of earlier centuries of European Christendom. And in the process, oft unwittingly, an utterly false cast is given the present strengths and weaknesses of religion in America.

It is no wonder that Americans so often misunderstand the relation of church and society appropriate to our situation, when so much of the scholarly treatment of church history neglects or misinterprets the American phase. As a president of the American Society of Church History protested several years ago,

> We cannot forever solve the problem of a right approach to church history by setting aside the experience of the American church as an anomaly.[9]

The primary purpose of this essay is to discuss the development of the American churches from the established Protestantism of the colonial state churches to the "post-Protestant" era in which Catholic-Protestant-Jewish trialogue is opening up new possibilities of theological clarification and articulation. In the process, however, some new light will be shed too on the political and social forces sustaining our democracy. This is not to say that sound religion is primarily directed to support of any political order; nevertheless sound religion is no mean asset to any nation, and some of the derivative values of a healthy church life may be of great significance. The pressing of self-analysis and self-discovery in the religious bodies may have, therefore, considerable value in clarifying some cultural, social, and political issues.

[9] Trinterud, L. J., "The Task of the American Church Historian," XXV *Church History* (1956) 1:3–15, 9.

In some conservative centers of "Christendom" it is common for the charge to be made that the Free Churches and voluntary religious associations have had little regard to natural law and the problems of general civic responsibility. This is usually related to the typology made popular by Ernst Troeltsch in *The Social Teaching of the Christian Churches* (English edition, 1931), in distinguishing the socially responsible "church" from the presumably irresponsible "sects." (The Jews are relegated to the limbo of neglect in this discussion.) As suggestive as this typology is sociologically, theologically it is pernicious. Any definition of the "church" which makes the church before Constantine a "sect" and relegates most of the modern missionary movement and the churches outside European "Christendom" to the status of "sects" obviously leaves much to be desired.

In point of historical fact, the Anabaptists and radical Puritans contributed a substantial portion of those understandings of religious liberty, voluntary association, separation of religious covenant from the political contract, stubborn attention to the reserved rights of subjects or citizens, and due process of law, which are of the highest qualities in the American experiment in self-government. The Anabaptist martyr Michael Sattler (1531) firmly protested that he was being persecuted and sentenced contrary to his rights as a subject of the Emperor. In a famous case involving the Quaker William Penn a century and a half later, the judge attempted to intimidate the jury by fining them for not entering the verdict he desired; the jury sued and won on a point of "due process." In the American colonies the Quakers and Baptists were just as vocal on their rights as Englishmen as they were in condemnation of the apostasy of Christendom—"the Vanity of this World, and the Irreligiousness of the Religions of it . . ."[10]

The truth is that there is more to social and civic responsibility than the mere verbalization of it, and some of those men and movements whose attention was devoted first to the restitution of the True Church were far more sensitive to political rights and reform than were those who

[10] Jacob, Caroline N., *Builders of the Quaker Road* (Chicago: Henry Regnery Co., 1953), p. 50.

ostensibly neglected the former for the sake of the latter, and in fact contributed little to either.

As we come to the modern period, where Protestant bodies with traditional apologetic ill adapted to voluntary-ism and pluralism are—like American Catholics and Jews—developing a style of internal life and public practice mark-edly different from that of the Old World, we shall again find unexpected strengths—political as well as religious—in the voluntary pattern. Within the next quarter century it will be decided for American Protestantism, at least, whether a new lease on life and spiritual energy can be un-leashed or whether it will sink back to be the sullen reli-gion of a declining minority with eyes fixed on the past.

The whole image of early America as a "Christian na-tion" (i.e. Protestant-controlled) is a lie which must be struck down: America was, in her colonial period—like con-tinental Europe—officially religious and in fact character-ized by "baptized heathenism"; in her early years as a nation she was overwhelmingly unchurched and heathen, regardless of pretensions and public claims. Today a larger percentage of her population is voluntarily churched, in Catholic, Protestant, and Jewish congregations, than ever before in her history. Whether this promising and problem-atical situation bodes good or ill depends upon whether Americans can come to a right perspective on their religious situation, regardless of their denomination or faith. To ac-quire a right perspective, and act upon it, we must abandon the anxieties which have so often in the past driven us into our respective ghettos, and accept with confidence and joy the given situation in which we are called to live and witness.

For the author's part, as a convinced evangelical Chris-tian he counts himself more at one with the believing Cath-olic or Jew than with those Protestants who long for the good old days and are in fact Protestants only because they have never contemplated the winsomeness of the alter-natives.

Easter, 1961. F. H. L.

CHAPTER I

The Colonial State Churches

Most of the European writings in church history still treat American religious life as a footnote to the history of European Christendom. This "footnote" was added out of charity, since the tremendous variety of religious societies in the United States simply demonstrated to the Continental that religious freedom resulted in anarchy and sectarianism. Only recently, under the impress of the ecumenical movement, have a few universities on the Continent begun to pay attention to the burgeoning vitality and strength of the "Younger Churches" of North America, Africa, Asia, and the islands of the sea. What the European scholars have not yet recognized is the fact that, although the American churches were once colonies of European Christendom, today the religious life in the U.S.A. is different in kind from that of the early period. It is not surprising, however, that the European intellectuals should treat church life in America as an unimportant appendix to the mother churches: most American seminaries still do exactly the same thing. American church history is also neglected in the seminaries of this country, and the church views of the sixteenth-century state-church reformers are proclaimed as sturdily as if they actually had controlling significance for the twentieth-century American religious setting.

The Latin Church

The first Christian religion planted in North America was that of the Latin Church, before Roman Catholicism had been defined at the Council of Trent (1545–63) or Lutheranism had been proclaimed in the Formula of Concord (1577) and Book of Concord (1580) or Calvinism had been crystallized in the Canons of the Synod of Dort (1618–19). Although the Reformation broke soon after the establishment of Spanish hegemony in the area surrounding the Gulf of Mexico (as well as Central and South America), the Inquisition and the Index were successful in suppressing even the influence of the Catholic Reformers overseas. The peculiar character of Latin American Catholicism to this day is primarily due to the fact that—unlike the Catholicism of Europe—it never went through the purifying agony of the Catholic Reformation. It remained, and remains to this day, essentially pre-sixteenth century.

There are important sections of the citizenry of the U.S.A., primarily in Puerto Rico, the Southwest, and southern California, who trace their church affiliation to the days of the Spanish empire. There are glorious pages of American church history which were written by Christian men of the stature and gifts of Father Junípero Serra (1713–84), Franciscan missionary in California. It was not until the cession of the Mississippi Valley to Napoleon, with subsequent sale to the American republic (1803), that it was determined finally that Anglo-American religious style would predominate in the area of the Great Plains. The fate of the areas comprising Florida, Texas, New Mexico, Arizona, and California was not settled until a generation (1821–45) after the east coast colonies established their independence. The natives of Puerto Rico did not acquire American citizenship, and thereby free movement to the continent, until the end of the nineteenth century.

Even more important as a political force, though the religious and cultural deposits in the contemporary U.S.A. are less significant, was the French Empire. All during the eighteenth century the French controlled Canada, the old Northwest, the upper Mississippi. During this time the magnificent record of French Catholic missions to the Indians was set. Some of the noblest martyrs of the expansion of Christianity were counted among the Jesuit missionaries to North America: Fathers Jogues (1607–46) and Brébeuf (1593–1649) were among the finest, and have been canonized. It was not until the French and Indian Wars of 1756–63 that French imperial power was reduced and English hegemony established. Until that time it seemed more than probable that the English colonies would be held to the area east of the Alleghenies. The chief deposit of French religious tradition is the province of Quebec, so vital to Canadian church history, although there was a period of years in the middle of the nineteenth century when it seemed possible that Louis Riel and his Métis might establish an empire in the Great Plains west of the Red River—combining parts of Canada and the north central states in a new French Catholic nation.

English Christendom

Thus it was finally determined, at the midpoint of our history, that the Anglo-Saxon tradition should predominate politically and religiously in the formative period. Such expansion as should occur would inevitably follow the political, legal, educational, and religious lines of the original English settlements. But even here the major transition was not settled, the transition which gave American religious life its peculiar style and flavor. For English colonial governments were paralleled by colonial churches: for half of American history, the churches were in fact but minor deposits of European Christendom—primarily that of the British Isles. The great break in American church life came at the midway mark, with disestablishment of the state churches. From that point on, America was primarily a mission field, the voluntary adherents were "new Christians," and the churches belonged to the category of "Younger Churches" rather than old-style "Christendom."

This shift occurred about the time when the surge of the English westward was beginning to be most pronounced. Thus the shift from state-church to free-church pattern was almost coincident with the opening of the challenge of the western frontier. As English-American religion moved westward into the Mississippi Valley and area of the Great Plains, it adopted more and more the basic style appropriate to churches formed by evangelism and voluntary affiliation. In the old states, on the other hand—and particularly in the Southeast, where industrialization and mobility of population came only with the Second World War, there has been a marked carry-over of state-church mentality to the present day.

In the meantime, in struggling to create a kind of self-consciousness in the American churches, there has been a pronounced tendency to read back into the colonial state churches views of religious liberty and voluntaryism which only a few isolated prophets in fact possessed. Not Roger Williams and William Penn dominated the colonial churches, but John Endicott and Sir William Berkeley.

We have grown accustomed to honor the founders of America as champions of liberty. Some of them, to be sure, sacrificed greatly to find a haven in the New World. For many, however, conditions were so undesirable in the Old World that abandonment of the past was more risky than burdensome. And most certainly, in creating a myth, we have come to read back into the past understandings of the nature of liberty which were but glimpsed in earlier generations and have not been permanently fixed even yet. Nowhere is this more true than in the field of religion. We have underestimated the extent to which religious life in America but mirrored the familiar lines of European Christendom. Even today our thinking is still dominated by theoretical and practical considerations which reflect the relations of cult and culture, religion and politics, church and state, which mark the former center of world power, while the actual situation goes undescribed and unmastered.

The first settlements in North America simply transplanted the religious concepts and practices of Europe, modifying them only when frontier conditions required adaptation and adjustment. For over half of our history American church life was modeled on European lines. The colonial state churches were as truly colonial dependencies as were the political units. Churches established and supported by law tend to swing between extremes of repression and latitudinarian policy. This has been the record in Europe and was the record in state-church Colonial America. In the one case confessional orthodoxy is maintained by suppressing nonconformity and persecuting "heresy." In the other, a policy of inclusiveness is pursued because discordant elements cannot be brought into harmony. Given a minimum of formal liturgical or confession agreement, widespread latitude is allowed in other matters. In either case, true religion is suppressed or ignored. The actual function of the church is then to perform a social function, i.e., to help to hold the society together.

New England

In New England, the attempt was made to organize all of social life under the lordship of Jesus Christ. Although commercial (fishing) enterprise was important from the start, and the "Gentiles" outnumbered the faithful before the colonies had counted thirty years, the Pilgrims and Puritans intended to establish a theocracy in which all civil and social decisions should be dominated by religion and religious leaders. The experiment which had collapsed at Geneva with the death of John Calvin was to be carried through in the New England standing order. The effort of clerical and lay leaders was so ruthlessly logical and intolerant of dissent that Oliver Cromwell and other key figures in the English Commonwealth (1640–58) were openly critical.

Plymouth was established in 1620, by a mixed company of gentlemen and indentured servants. The former, having grown anxious during their period of refuge in the Netherlands lest their children begin to wed out in the world, sought a frontier where they could worship and serve God according to conviction and without accommodation. Religious liberty, though implicit in their style of thinking about the church, was not their aim: they sought liberty for themselves, not for all. The Mayflower Compact, actually twofold in character, was radical Puritan and democratic in implication but not in intent. In forming their covenant, joined in and supported by all qualified persons, the Pilgrim fathers distinguished between the religious and the civil covenants. But after landing, faced by starvation and disease, they reverted to a monolithic structure and policy. "Heresy" was harried out of the land, and the Indians who clung to their ancient rights and property were driven before the front of white European civilization. Neither Anne Hutchinson, the lay prophetess, nor "King" Philip, the Indian chief, found understanding or charity at the hands of the Lord's anointed. Although, on the basis of what they had learned as non-conformists in England and exiles in Holland, the Pilgrims knew to distinguish between that covenant which unites the faithful of the churches and the civil compact which binds fellow citizens, in practice they reverted to a continuum of religion and politics.

When Massachusetts Bay Colony was established a few years later, the mood of the founders was different. They did not come out joyfully, damning England as a cage of all unclean birds, but with hearts of loyalty toward the mother country. They were conservative Puritans, who had hoped to turn the established Church of England into a presbyterial rather than episcopal system. When it became clear that the Stuarts would hold to James I's utterance at Hampton Court (1604)—"No bishop, no king!"—they turned reluctantly to the New World to find religious freedom. But it was freedom for their own program, not for all.

As New England developed, the inconsistency between a congregational church view which pointed toward initiative and voluntaryism and the determination to restrict political and religious authority to the Saints became more acute. On the side of voluntaryism and lay initiative, within a generation the churches in Massachusetts Bay adopted the custom of using the Church Covenant. In this they pledged with God and each other to follow the pilgrim way, whatever it should cost. On the page of the ledger headed "European Christendom," the parish plan was maintained, and the church property was held by township rather than by covenanting congregation. In the end, this brought disaster to the New England church order: following the Dedham Case (1819–20), the Trinitarian Congregationalists lost to the Unitarian Congregationalists all but a handful of church properties within fifty miles of Boston. By 1833 the inconsistencies of the situation were apparent enough to lead to a willingness on the part of Massachusetts Christendom to abandon state-church ways. The last appropriation of tax monies to support Christian (Unitarian) and theological education at Harvard was made in 1834. Connecticut had taken the step toward religious liberty in 1819.

The point to remember, however, is that the New England standing order shattered on an inconsistency which ran back to its founding. A pilgrim church cannot be a successful establishment. A church which stresses membership confirmed by live faith and fortified by internal discipline cannot include the whole population in its regimen. Yet it was understandable that in the rigorous life of the frontier the Christians should revert to the pattern of control which had obtained for over a millennium of church history.

An Example of Puritan Statecraft: The Christian Indian Villages

The story of the Christian Indian villages affords one of the most wistful chapters in American church history, and at the same time it records at the end the first of a long line of ignominious failures in white Christendom's approach to the original inhabitants of the land. The failures have been due to the general inability of white American Christians to distinguish between their tribal mores and culture and the essential matters of the faith. The failure of American society vis-à-vis the American Indians is in this respect but another body of proof that American religion has remained largely committed to the stance of European Christendom rather than moving out imaginatively in the spirit and style of a triumphant evangelism. In spite of the myth of "separation," American Protestantism has persistently required that converts of the missions should adopt the food, housing, clothing, social patterns, property ownership, and cultural values of white western civilization.

The New England experiment with the Christian Indian villages shows both the struggles and weaknesses of Puritan civilization as it flowered in the New World. The mind-set which was later to rule the scattered Puritan settlements of the old Middle West and southern Bible Belt, leading to the reactions so well known by the writings of H. L. Mencken, Sherwood Anderson, and Thomas Wolfe, was already evident when John Eliot began his great civilizing work among the Indian tribes of old New England. There is no better model for the study of Puritan statecraft, for the Indian converts were uprooted and had to be re-formed and re-ordered from the ground up. They had been evicted from the tribal structure for adopting the white man's religion. They had no social or political order that the Europeans recognized. They were filled with an unbounded admiration for the settlers' houses, weapons, and gods. By the end of the first generation the Puritan commonwealth was already threatened by white settlers who challenged its politics and its creeds. Not so the Christian Indians: they could be shaped utterly and finally according to the stern logic of Puritan statecraft. Never in Geneva, the Protectorate, or in white New England did the reverend fathers in God have such an opportunity to demonstrate what they could and would do with completely tractable material.

John Eliot (1604–90) was the godly and gifted man who translated the Bible into the Narragansett tongue, published it by section (the first Bible printed in the English colonies), and set out to order the converts according to the logic of his Puritan faith. For Eliot the congregational covenant was the apostolic and primitive.

. . . he looked upon a Relation unto a Church, as not a *Natural*, or a *Violent*, but a *Voluntary* thing, and so that it is to be entered no otherwise than by an Holy *Covenant*, or, as the Scripture speaks, by *giving our selves first unto the Lord, and then one unto another*.[1]

Thus it was that when the converts were of sufficient number, in a great meeting on the sixth day of the sixth month, 1651, Eliot led them in establishing their covenant in a great meeting.

We doe give our selves and our Children unto God to be his people, he shall rule us in all our affaires, not onely in our Religion, and affaires of the Church (these we desire as soone as we can if God will) but also in all our works and affaires in this World, God shall rule over us. Isa 33.22. The Lord is our Judge, the Lord is our Law-giver, the Lord is our King, He will save us; the Wisedome which God hath taught us in his Booke, that shall guide us and direct us in the way. Oh Jehovah, teach us Wisedome to finde out thy wisedome in Thy Scriptures, let the grace of Christ helpe us, because Christ is the wisedome of God, send Thy Spirit into our hearts, and let it teach us, Lord take us to be thy people, and let us take thee to be our God.[2]

This covenant is noteworthy for the inclusion of the children: already some of the radical Puritans were limiting accountability to those who had reached "the age of understanding." It is also noteworthy because, although in the Commonwealth the political covenant was already being separated from the religious, in this "control group" the civil and religious covenant were one. A theocracy was the

[1] Mather, Cotton, *The Life of the Renowned John Eliot* (Boston: Harris & Allen, 1691), p. 66.

[2] *Strength out of Weakness. Or a Glorious Manifestation of the Further Progresse of the Gospel amongst the Indians in New England* (London, 1652); reprinted for Joseph Sabin, New York, 1865: Quarto Series, No. V, pp. 14–15.

ideal, and the peoples were numbered by tens, fifties, hundreds. As Eliot later explained it, "There is undoubtedly a forme of Civil Government instituted by God himself in the holy scriptures."

> And this vow I did solemnly make unto the Lord concerning them; that they being a people without any forme of Government, and now to chuse; I would endeavour with all my might, to bring them under the Government of the Lord only: Namely, that I would instruct them to imbrace such government, both Civil and Ecclesiastical, as the Lord hath commanded in the holy Scriptures; and to deduce all their Laws from the holy Scriptures, that so they may be the Lords people, ruled by him alone in all things . . .[3]

The Commonwealth parliament was greatly pleased at the evidence of the daybreak of the gospel among the tribes, and chartered a society which collected and transmitted £4673 in ten years: "The Society for the Promoting and Propagating of the Gospel of Jesus Christ in New England." The villages were formed, first Natick and then nearly a dozen others. But tragedy was close at hand. In an appeal for separate settlements one of the converted chiefs had put the problem:

> . . . that because we pray to God, other *Indians* abroad in the country hate us and oppose us, the English on the other side suspect us, and feare us to be still such as doe not pray at all—.[4]

During the first of King Philip's War a corps of Christian Indians fought with the whites, but others were suspected and suffered greatly at the hands of the whites. At the end

[3] Eliot, John, *The Christian Commonwealth: or, The Civil Policy of the Rising Kingdom of Jesus Christ* (London: Livewell Chapman, 1659), *Preface.*

[4] Shepard, Thomas, *The Clear Sunshine of the Gospel Breaking Forth upon the Indians in New England* (London, 1648); reprinted for Joseph Sabin, New York, 1865: Quarto Series, No. X, p. 50.

many were sold off with the insurgents as slaves in the West Indies. The Christian Indian villages came to a miserable end, and by the time Eliot's Bible was finally available in the language, the Indians were gone who could have read it.

Later to be duplicated in the brutal suppression of the Moravian's Gnadenhütten, in the expropriation of the civilized nations by Georgia before the "March of Tears" westward, and at a dozen other points in American history, it was amply demonstrated from the beginning that the whites thought of Christianity as the white man's religion—as a function of Western Christendom; and could neither understand nor trust the works of the Christian mission to the Indians.

Equally important is the fact that Eliot, determined "to carry on civility with religion,"[5] conceived of the Europeanization of the Indians as a fundamental part of the Christianization process. If a man of his breadth of vision could not see beyond the limits of white society, how much more astigmatic was the common view! On the two hundredth anniversary of the founding of Natick, Professor Calvin Stowe (Harriet Beecher Stowe's husband) spoke a wise word: "It is true, as someone has said, that the great majority of the Indians made but 'sorry Christians'; but this has always been equally true of the great majority of white men."[6] But the sins and weaknesses of the white men were easier for white men to put up with. The failure of the mission to the Indians was due to the fact that the vision of the whites did not as yet extend beyond European Christendom and its colonies.

As a study in Puritan statecraft the model experiment with the helpless Indians gives us an early clue of what kinds of controls Puritans might later institute in those vil-

[5] "Letters of Eliot," *Collections of the Massachusetts Historical Society* (Boston: Charles C. Little and James Brown, 1846), Series 3, Vol. IV, p. 88.

[6] Bacon, O., *A History of Natick* (Boston: Damrell & Moore, 1856), p. 253.

lages of the frontier where their authority was for a time supreme.

Religion in the Proprietary Colonies

Because there were periods when the proprietors of the colonies west and south of New England practiced toleration in order to attract and hold farmers, craftsmen and servants (primarily Dissenters) from the Old World, later writers have often underestimated the degree of arbitrary control exercised in behalf of the Church of England. Nevertheless, only Pennsylvania functioned consistently as a haven of refuge for the most various of dissenting groups, and even there acceptance of one God, Sabbath observance, and belief in Jesus were chartered requirements. Thomas Fitzsimons, an Irish Catholic active in the Continental Congress and Constitutional Convention, was kept from public office until the Revolution by the 1702 Test Oath; but he lived to serve in the 1790 Convention that established complete religious liberty.

From Maryland south to Georgia there were recurring periods of persecution and repression. More serious, perhaps, Anglican domination so influenced education and religio-political structures that when disestablishment came the cause of religion was set back for a generation.

In Maryland, the Calverts introduced toleration in order to satisfy their Puritan settlers. The latter turned in a later day to suppress the Catholicism of the proprietors. The religious issue was further confused by conflict in the charters granted the second Lord Baltimore and William Penn. With the transfer to royal authority, following a rebellion in the colony (1689), Anglicanism was established. Even after reversion of title to the Calvert family, which had in the meantime become Protestant, Catholics were disfranchised and repressed.

In Virginia, Anglicanism was established and sustained by taxes and levies from the first. When, largely as a result of the shift to voluntaryism which resulted from the Great Awakening, the fight for the Bill of Religious Freedom was launched, many patriots, notably George Washington and Patrick Henry, stood by the principle of establishment. Even Thomas Jefferson (1743–1826), who coined the famous and often misused phrase on the "wall of separation," no more believed in separating religion from public life than did his Federalist opponents in New England. As rector he enforced compulsory Protestant chapel at the State University of Virginia, a practice continued to the end of the Civil War. Two years before his death he attempted to meet the changing religious complexion of the students by inviting the religious bodies to establish "schools for instruction in the religion of their sect" and stated that if such denominational schools were established at the campus

> . . . the students of the University will be free, and expected to attend religious worship at the establishment of their respective sects, in the morning, and in time to meet their school in the University at its stated hour.[7]

This is of course nothing other than "released time," against which absolutists of the American Jewish Committee, Humanist Association, etc., have inveighed so resolutely. The policy may be unwise; the writer is convinced that there is much to be said against it, both practically and in principle in a pluralistic society. But the problem cannot be solved by rewriting historical facts and evidence. The Northwest Ordinance of 1787, based on Jefferson's land ordinance of 1784 and urging the cause of "religion, morality, and knowledge," comes closer to representing Jefferson's mind on the matter than phrases lifted out of context to prove him a twentieth-century secularist. And of the other great Virginians of the early years of the Republic there can be no doubt at all: they were all committed to the cause of organized religion—a few as supporters of the Great Awakening and voluntaryism, the large majority as taxpayers and patrons of the state church.

[7] Knight, Edward W., ed., *A Documentary History of Education in the South Before 1860* (Chapel Hill: University of North Carolina Press, 1942), III, 154.

Although the record was more erratic in the proprietary colonies than in New England, the major religious factor in most of the populated areas of the middle and southern settlements was also the established church. The record in South Carolina may be taken as representative of the way European "Christendom," Anglican form, functioned on American soil. In sum, it brought all of the problems which characterized its existence in the Old World, and few of the benefits.

From 1700 on the major political conflict in the colony was shaped up around the conflict of the Establishment and the Dissenters, with the latter growing in the back country and a pronounced drift to Anglicanism on the coast. In 1704 a bill was jammed through, 12 to 11, to exclude all Dissenters from the legislature; the "Anglicans" did not have to be faithful communicants however, but merely pledge that they were not Dissenters. When the Rev. Mr. Marston of St. Philip's parish denounced the hypocrisy, he too was forced into a fight for the liberty of the church. The assembly demanded his notes, sequestered his salary, and attempted to force him out of the colony; he replied that only the Bishop of London was his superior and that he would answer to him. In 1706 the Church Act was passed, with Dissenters excluded from voting; the land was divided into parishes, which from 1716 on were the geographical bases for membership in the assembly and which continued until 1865 to be the bases for South Carolina's judicial system. From 1706 to withdrawal of government aid in 1778 the Anglican clergy, frequently immoral and guilty of gross neglect of their people, shared a major part of the colony's budget: in 1722 nearly one fourth of the taxes went to the established church.

As the establishment lost public confidence and respect, coercion became more severe. For two decades prior to independence the dissenting clergy even lost the right to perform marriages. The result was as predictable as it was catastrophic: with independence came disestablishment, and the Anglican Church was left prostrate for a generation —with only two clergymen left in the new state for a time and no members trained in voluntary support. For many years, after a modest recovery like that in Virginia, the congregations kept the clergy on trial for many years before electing them in charge; many never did complete the process of installing a rector.[8] The way of the Protestant Episcopal Church was hard for generations; through the Civil War, at least, leadership passed to the Presbyterians. For a generation before the firing on Fort Sumter the Presbyterians dominated the State University and the state assembly. In the generation before that the Unitarians controlled the State University. Under date of October 27, 1835, John England, Bishop of Charleston, wrote Francis Lieber with reference to the disabilities he suffered as a Roman Catholic in a setting dominated by "a party which under the pretext of religion indulges in the malevolence of disappointed monopoly." After years of effort he had to conclude: "I found that my religion was never to be forgiven."

In a state with such a tradition, the Dissenters readily reverted to the state-church pattern when their turn came to determine public policy. Such was the use Unitarians and Presbyterians made of power when they had it. The influence of Baptists and Methodists has been exerted at times in the same way, notably in legislation during the anti-saloon, anti-evolution and anti-communist flurries. Protestant chapel services, led by a Protestant chaplain, were held regularly on campus through World War II, and the University has not yet officially accepted the pluralistic pattern of student religious life.

In colonial Georgia the establishment was less oppressive but none the less real. Roman Catholics were excluded by the 1732 charter. The Moravians were persecuted for refusal to bear arms during the Spanish threat, 1737, and left in 1740 for Pennsylvania. Many Jews left the same year because of difficulties and disabilities suffered. In 1754 the colony reverted to the status of a royal province and several efforts were made to enforce the Anglican establishment.

[8] Wallace, David Duncan, *South Carolina: A Short History, 1520–1948* (Chapel Hill: University of North Carolina Press, 1951), esp. Chapters IX and XXIII.

One of the ministers of the Salzburgers plead with the legislators to remember

> . . . that the Province of Georgia was intended by his Majesty for an asylum for all sorts of Protestants to enjoy full liberty of Conscience Preferable to any other American Colonies in order to invite members of Oppressed or persecuted People to strengthen this barrier Colony by their coming over.[9]

But the law of Anglican establishment was passed, 1758, and eight parishes became the official religious organs of the colony and the governmental as well—for fire fighting, civil guards, justices of the peace, street-cleaning supervisors, etc. By 1773 one third of the legislators were dissenters, properly resenting having to pay fees to the Anglican rector for burying their own dead. George Whitefield, the great preacher of the Awakening, had to abandon his plans for a college: he got the land but the charter stipulated an Anglican president and daily services. When, with statehood, the Constitution of 1798 was written, provision was made for complete religious liberty including Roman Catholics. It was more than a generation before the newly formed Protestant Episcopal Church began to recover from the costs of earlier privilege.

Although Georgia was less significant in numbers than the Carolinas or Virginia, her situation on the southern frontier with Spain made her religious and military condition important in the new nation. As a colony she had had an Anglican establishment but no heavy record of persecution of dissenters. Nevertheless, she paid the price of formal establishment in decline of true religion and membership loyalty.

In 1786, with 80,000 whites and Negroes in the new state there were not over five hundred active Christians in all; there were three Episcopal parishes without rectors and three Lutheran churches, three Presbyterian churches,

[9] *American Colonial Tracts* (Rochester, N.Y.: George P. Humphrey, n.d.), XIII, 257–59.

three Baptist churches—all small and all struggling.[10] This is not unrepresentative of the situation in the proprietary colonies generally, where the establishment was simply unfitted to the needs of an expanding population and only militant home missions of the type developed by the radical wing of Protestantism were capable of meeting the challenge. In the first years of statehood, when "the leading men of the state were duellists and infidels," the future of self-government was racked by a major swindle involving the western lands—the Yazoo Scandal, which drew leading men of Georgia and the Southeast into corrupt speculation and sale of the area later to be Alabama and Mississippi. The reclaiming of the state for active religion began with the revivals of 1802 and 1806, in which the Camp Meeting first came into use.

In sum, we have a colonial record in New England with an oppressive establishment of mixed Congregational and Presbyterian order, with an internal inconsistency carrying the seeds of its own destruction. In the southern colonies, Anglicanism enjoyed up to the time of the Revolution a position of privilege which—when it collapsed—left whole sections of the population unchurched. In New York State the picture was more ambiguous, although both Friends and Presbyterians were compelled to fight for their rights under the Anglican establishment. Only in Pennsylvania, and the colonies which for some time shared its history (the Jerseys and Delaware), was the shift to religious liberty and voluntary support accomplished without severe readjustment. Pennsylvania, indeed, despised by New Englanders and southerners alike as a "swamp of sectarianism," foreshadowed in its religious life the variety and lay activism which were later to become characteristic of the whole American religious scene.

[10] Smith, Geo. G., *The History of Georgia Methodism* (Atlanta: A. B. Caldwell, Publ., 1913), Chapter I.

The Great Awakening

Although revivalism began in New Jersey under the preaching of the Dutch Pietist, Domine Freylinghausen, its consequences can be divined most readily by considering the career of Jonathan Edwards and the effect of the Wesleyan revivals in the southern colonies.

Jonathan Edwards (1703–58), in the colonial years the greatest and most creative of American theologians, symbolizes the beginning of the transition from establishment to voluntaryism. Even though he opposed assertion of lay authority because of his confidence in the standing order and its structure, his emphasis on conversion and articulated religious experience—like his doctrines of grace and church discipline—pointed toward a more live initiative on the part of the whole people of God. Even though the state church hung on for three more generations in Massachusetts, it was the forces of voluntaryism which Edwards saw and welcomed in the Great Awakening which forecast its eventual dissolution. Against Charles Chauncey and the other champions of gentlemanly and cultured religion Edwards urged the power of God to break in and make new men and women of the roughest material. Against the self-satisfaction of the "good people," secure in their own "righteousness," who controlled his own congregation at Northampton, he pressed the scriptural passage which Anabaptists and radical Puritans used as proof text for church discipline (Matt. 18:15–18).

Both the Lesser Ban, "fencing the table" (permitting only those in good standing to take Communion) and the Greater Ban (expulsion) point toward voluntary church membership with discipline. No state church has ever been able to maintain church discipline, although occasionally the effort has been made to introduce it. For his efforts Jonathan Edwards, the most distinguished theologian and preacher of his age and section, was dismissed summarily from the pulpit that his grandfather and he had served a total of eighty-one years and allowed to settle in the western wilderness as missionary to the Indians of Stockbridge. The good people of the good parishes of New England's state churches were not ready to accept a standard of Christian faith and practice which required more than the casual claims of culture-religion. Or, to speak more generally, the decline of the theocratic drive of earlier years of the establishment had left a situation in which religion was conceived as a desirable cultural force and pillar of the social order rather than a consuming fire in which to mold new men and women.

The career of Edwards shows the inevitable conflict between an evangelism pointing toward voluntaryism and initiative and a parish system resting upon traditional Christendom. The conflict is often stated in theological terms alone as a conflict between Arminianism and orthodoxy, with the result that the structural situation is obscured. But George Whitefield (1714–70), who toured the colonies from one end to the other as a traveling evangelist, was as strong a Calvinist as Edwards. Neither could escape the fact that an evangelical proclamation calls for decision, and decision calls for lay initiative; lay initiative points toward voluntary discipline and support, not toward content with religion as one of several departments of life.

The Great Awakening must be conceived as the first major manifestation of a motif which, more than any other, has shaped modern American church life: mass evangelism. Even though the camp meeting had not yet appeared, and other carefully planned techniques of the later evangelism had not become routine, the Great Awakening was a forecast of things to come. The New England establishment resisted the Great Awakening fairly successfully, sacrificing even Jonathan Edwards to the commitments of culture-religion. Even late in the nineteenth century there were still discriminatory clauses in New England state constitutions. In the South, however, the Awakening carried right up to the Revolutionary War. By the time the new states were writing their constitutions and proclaiming religious liberty, the revival emphasis was already fairly advanced in Methodist, Baptist, and "New Side" Presbyterian circles.

The work which had begun in an effort to enliven a stagnant Christendom was now carried forward as an offensive to reclaim the people for the church on a voluntary basis. This is the primary distinction between the Great Awakening and later revivals, between the Second Great Awakening in Connecticut and the contemporary impulse in the Cane Ridge Revival in Kentucky: in one case the revivals were functioning within the setting of a reluctant and even resistant "Christendom," in the other, evangelism had blended with that characteristically American institution, "Home Missions," of which the European establishments have no counterpart to this day.

From the time of the Great Awakening (1734 ff.) on, the revivalist wing of the Presbyterians and the Methodists began to play an increasingly important role in American religious life. Of the two, the Presbyterians were at first more significant. In New England, the conservative order resisted revivalism and the faculties at Harvard and Yale finally pronounced against it. In the middle colonies, however, the situation of the Scotch-Irish on the frontier called for new methods and warm zeal lest the scattered settlers be lost permanently to the Christian cause. Under the leadership of the Tennents, father and son, some Presbyterians endeavored to respond to the need—even if it meant using preachers not fully up to the fixed standards of the Synod. In the division which occurred, 1741, the "New Side" founded Princeton and grew rapidly in the newer settlements.

This was but the first of many divisions which revivalism has brought in the course of American Presbyterian history and one of the soonest healed. With reunion in 1758 the Presbyterian movement expanded dramatically in the southern states. The ministers, with their committees of correspondence planning religious advance across colony lines, and with their resolute opposition to ecclesiastical actions taken or threatened by the English crown, played a very significant role in the development of a national consciousness and in the battle for independence. Indeed, it might be claimed that the organization of concerted effort for the evangelization of the people drifting from the eastern parishes into the unchurched areas, and the planning of a series of revival campaigns, opened up the first channel through which men thought and felt and acted as "Americans" rather than as subjects in individual colonies.

In the mission to the de-churched the Methodists played an enlarging role with the Great Awakening in the southern (Anglican) colonies. Although hampered by John Wesley's reluctance and delay in ordaining ministers for America and by widespread Tory sentiments in the ranks of the itinerants, Methodism under Francis Asbury (1745–1816) grew rapidly during the 1770s, regrouped with efficiency after the war (in 1784), and by the time of Wesley's death (1791) numbered 43,265 members in the United States. The peculiar institutions of Methodism—itinerancy, lay preaching, and the class meeting—were all eminently fitted to work in frontier conditions. Asbury himself traveled from Maine to the Gulf, as far west as the Mississippi, ordained some 3000 preachers and preached about 17,000 sermons in his lifetime of heroic leadership.

During the same period, the Baptists also came to the fore. In the most vigorous period of the New England establishment, Baptists suffered whippings, jailings, and other persecutions. During the Great Awakening, however, many supporters of the revival were forced out of state-church parishes and joined the Baptists: growth was particularly rapid in New England and Virginia and North Carolina. As with the Methodists, however, the great flowering of Baptist strength came with the westward movement which followed the Revolutionary War and swelled throughout the first half of the nineteenth century. In the battle for religious freedom in Virginia it was a combination of Baptist and Presbyterian forces that carried the victory.

With independence, the Anglican state churches collapsed overnight. As there had never been a bishop in the colonies, the tendency had long been for power to shift to the vestries. Indeed, in some respects the Anglican parishes were as Puritan in doctrine and organization as the parishes of New England. The latter, however, withstood more sturdily the shock of the establishment of a national government deliberately neutral on religious matters. The state churches of New England continued for a generation after independence, and in some areas of the middle west the particular style of New England Puritanism survived into the twentieth century.

The Rise of Dissent

From the beginning there was that within the New England order which pointed toward its ultimate disintegration. When Roger Williams (1607–84), protégé of Sir Edward Coke and friend of Oliver Cromwell, arrived in the New World the incoherences between a congregationalist effort to restore the New Testament church and a presbyterian parish system were already apparent. On two different occasions (1631 and 1633) he attempted to work out the plan of a covenanting congregation with the Salem Church, only to be resisted, tried, and finally expelled by the General Court—which was at that time sturdily committed to the parish system of appointment and support. Expelled from the Bay Colony, after a temporary respite at Plymouth he went on to found the Providence Plantations on the basis of "soul liberty." Here Quakers and Baptists were to find refuge from persecution by the orthodox of the state churches.

The case of Anne Hutchinson (1590–1643) is equally revealing. She has generally been condemned as an "Antinomian" heretic by defenders of the political action which sent her to exile and death. Actually, she seems to have stood in the radical Puritan tradition. Against the stern scholasticism of the established order she proclaimed the work of the Holy Spirit and the joyful fruits of faith and love. Against the clerical monopoly she proclaimed and displayed the "irregularities" of lay initiative and Biblical interpretation. In 1637 she was confronted by the combined forces of the political and clerical rulers of the colony, charged with eighty-two doctrinal errors, and banished. At this distance it is apparent that the rulers of the standing order were most disturbed by the effrontery of a lay woman who presumed to express opinions on matters reserved to a professional class of ministers who combined theological orthodoxy with status as civil servants. At the height of her popularity Mrs. Hutchinson had the support of many of the leading citizens of the Boston church—including John Cotton and the governor, Sir Henry Vane.

Vane (?–1662) was one of the noblest champions of open inquiry and religious liberty in New England history, and was forced out of office (1637) as a result and in spite of his major accomplishments in military and Indian affairs. Returning to England, he was instrumental in securing a charter for Rhode Island. In his honor John Milton penned a fine sonnet (XVII):

> *. . . besides to know*
> *Both spirituall powre and civill, what each meanes*
> *What severs each thou hast learnt, which few have don.*
> *The bounds of either sword to thee wee ow.*
> *Therfore on thy firme hand religion leanes*
> *In peace, & reck'ns thee her eldest son.*

At the time of the Commonwealth there was considerably greater sensitivity to religious liberty in England than in Puritan New England.

The last to pay the price of opposition to the Puritan state church were the Quakers and Baptists. Against the former, the pious brought the most frightful traditional penalties of European Christendom. The latter, coming to flower following on the Great Awakening, carried away a whole harvest of covenanting congregations who shifted from the inconsistences of a congregationalism unequally yoked to state power to a clear espousal of voluntary association and support.

The Travelling Friends were savagely persecuted by the magistrates of Massachusetts. When Anne Hutchinson was excommunicated and expelled in a state-church ceremony, Mary Dyer arose and walked down the aisle and out with her. Returning three times in spite of warnings and punishments, she was hanged as a Quaker. In May 1661, branding with the letter R and this further were added: that the Quaker should be "stripped naked from the middle upwards, and tied to a cart's tail, and whipped through the town."[11] Four were hanged, a number whipped; others had ears cut off, or were branded. On May 11, 1659, the General Court of Election of Boston gave authority for the sale of the son and daughter of Lawrence Southwick, Quaker, to the Barbadoes as slaves.[12]

It is of first importance that in the midst of all this the Quakers repeatedly made claim to their rights as Englishmen, against persecution for any preaching. Thus in the case of Wenlock Christian, it is given:

Wenlock: 'By what law will you put me to death?'

Court: 'We have a law, and by our law, you are to die.'

Wenlock: 'So said the Jews of Christ, we have a law, and by our law he ought to die. Who empowered you to make that law?'

Court: 'We have a patent and are patentees; judge whether we have not power to make laws?'

Wenlock: 'How! have you power to make laws repugnant to the laws of England?'

Endicott: 'Nay.'

Wenlock: 'Then you have gone beyond your bounds, and have forfeited your patent, and this is more than you can answer. Are you subjects to the king, yea or nay?'

Rawson: 'What will you infer from that, what good will that do you?'

Wenlock: 'If you are, say so: for in your petition to the king, you desire that he will protect you, and that you may be worthy to kneel among his royal subjects?'

Court: 'Yes.'

[11] Hallowell, Richard P., *The Pioneer Quakers* (Boston: Houghton Mifflin Co., 1887), pp. 48–49.

[12] Hallowell, Richard P., *The Quaker Invasion of Massachusetts* (Boston: Houghton Mifflin Co., 1883), p. 175.

Wenlock: 'So am I, and for any thing I know, am as good as you, if not better, for if the king did but know your hearts, as God knows them, he would see that your hearts are as rotten towards him as they are towards God. Therefore seeing that you and I are subjects to the king, I demand to be tried by the laws of my own nation.'

Court: 'You shall be tried by a bench and jury.'

Wenlock: 'That is not the law, but the manner of it: if you will be as good as your word, you must set me at liberty, for I never heard or read of any law that was in England to hang Quakers.'

Endicott: 'There is a law to hang Jesuits.'

Wenlock: 'If you put me to death, it is not because I go under the name of a Jesuit, but a Quaker; therefore I appeal to the laws of my own nation.'

Court: 'You are in our hands, and have broken our laws, and we will try you.'

Wenlock: 'Your will is your law, and what you have power to do, *that* you will do; and seeing that the jury must go forth on my life, this I have to say to you in the fear of the living God: "Jury, take heed what you do, for you swear by the living God, that you will true trial make, and just verdict give, according to the evidence; What have I done to deserve death? Keep your hands out of innocent blood."'

A Juryman: 'It is good counsel.'[13]

And the jury refused to pronounce sentence, and only by threats were induced to bring a verdict of guilty; Endicott had to read it out himself.

Major-General Denison had met the Quaker plea for rights with the remark "This year you will go and complain to Parliament, and the next year they will send out to see how it is, and the third year the government will be

[13] Bowden, James, A *History of the Society of Friends in America* (London: W. & F. G. Cash, 1850–54), I, 223–24.

changed!" The king heard of it, and about the same time received a list of wrongs against the Quakers:[14]

1. Two honest and innocent women stripped stark naked and searched in an inhuman manner.

2. Twelve strangers in that country, but freeborn of this nation, received twenty-three whippings, most of them with a whip of three cords with knots at the ends.

3. Eighteen inhabitants of the country, being free-born English, received twenty-three whippings.

4. Sixty-four imprisonments of 'the Lord's people', amounting to five hundred and nineteen weeks.

5. Two beaten with pitched ropes, the blows amounting to an hundred and thirty-nine.

6. An innocent old man banished from his wife and children, and for returning put in prison for above a year.

7. Twenty-five banished upon penalties of being whipped, or having their ears cut, or a hand branded.

8. Fines, amounting to a thousand pounds, laid upon the inhabitants for meeting together.

9. Five kept fifteen days without food.

10. One laid neck and heels in irons for sixteen hours.

11. One very deeply burnt in the right hand with an H after he had been beaten with thirty stripes.

12. One chained to a log of wood for the most part of twenty days in winter time.

13. Five appeals to England denied.

14. Three had their right ears cropped off.

15. One inhabitant of Salem, since banished on pain of death, had one-half of his house and land seized.

16. Two ordered sold as bond-servants.

17. Eighteen of the people of God banished on pain of death.

---

[14] Jones, Rufus M., Sharpless, Isaac, Gummere, Amelia M., *The Quakers in the American Colonies* (London: Macmillan Co., 1923), pp. 91-92.

18. Three of the servants of God put to death. (Wm. Leddra was executed after this was written.)

19. Since the executions four more banished on pain of death and twenty-four heavily fined for meeting to worship God.

His *Missive,* popularized by Whittier's poem, saved Wenlock Christian's life, and loosened the repressive measures. Although the following year they were returned, without the death penalty, the regard of more tolerant neighbors and growing feeling within the colony combined to relieve the pressure.

New England had entered the time of the Half-Way Covenant, and Quakerism had left the period of martyrdom for the period of colonization. There were meetings of strength, by 1700, in all of the colonies; there were six Yearly Meetings—Rhode Island, 1661; Baltimore, 1672; Virginia, 1673; Burlington–Philadelphia, 1681; New York, 1696; and North Carolina, 1698. Half a century later there were more Quakers in America than in England.

During the Great Awakening some congregations separated to join the Baptists, and in others members were forced out for "enthusiasm." Separate churches were already allowed, although all paid taxes to the establishment. With the turn of the century Connecticut had become the chief bulwark of the theocratic approach. Only the danger of losing the colonial charter, in 1756, provided a let up. It was the fight against an Anglican episcopate for America which helped Baptists and other separatists to gain public standing. This, and general resentment of the Quebec Act (1774), which granted recognition and toleration to French Canadians, united the Free Churches and the established parishes against common enemies. Yet, in Connecticut, the defenders of the standing order hung on to the last. In 1816 a last desperate bid was made, with a Bill for Support of Literature and Religion apportioned as follows: Yale—$68,000, Episcopalians—$20,000, Methodists—$12,-000, Baptists—$18,000; the hope of the conservatives was to achieve the support of the larger denominations for a pluralistic establishment. But in 1818 the party of religious liberty won out, by a 105 to 95 majority.

From a legal point of view, New Hampshire carried on the tradition of the establishment most resolutely—even after Connecticut and Massachusetts had yielded and gone over to voluntaryism. The convention of 1792 still restricted the franchise. In 1804 the Freewill Baptists were granted toleration, in 1805 the Universalists. As late as 1850, however, after numerous immigrants had entered the state from Quebec, Catholic emancipation was overwhelmingly defeated. In 1877 a state convention was still debating omitting "Protestant" from the Bill of Rights. In 1902 the word was changed to "Christian," and that was retained in 1912 by voters' referendum in spite of strong protest against discrimination against the Jews.

Although Lyman Beecher fought against Connecticut disestablishment in 1818–19, he later admitted it was the happiest day for the churches when the shift to home missions and voluntary support and discipline was accomplished. In Massachusetts, the change was not made until wholesale losses to the Unitarians had occurred. In all of this period, the dissenting churchmen were subject to varying disabilities both political and social. Rather than reading back into the New England tradition a principle of religious liberty which did not exist until fairly late, and then reluctantly, we would do well to realize that where New England Puritanism has been transplanted to the West and South its tendency consistently has been coercive.

CHAPTER II

The New Nation

The American colonists won their independence with a population of approximately three and a half million, of whom only about 20,000 were Roman Catholics and 6000 Jews. Formally, the new nation was a "Christian nation," and for most this meant a Protestant nation. This image has persisted to the present day, in spite of ample statistical evidence that the established Protestant churches by no means commanded the loyalty or willing support of the vast majority of the population. In fact, however, the new nation was a heathen nation—one of the most needy mission fields in the world. And for the major part of the nineteenth century, Protestant and Catholic missionary societies in Europe were sending to it missionaries, tracts, and money to save the New World from relapse into utter irreligion.

Nor did the peculiar conditions of the frontier create the only area where Christianity was challenged. Among the older coastal settlements the crisis was also acute. Indeed, over all, when the colonial state churches collapsed, church membership fell to its true percentage. In the southern colonies it took thirty years and more for the Anglican church to get back on its feet. In the middle colonies the Great Awakening carried on right up to the Revolution. In New England, leaders tried hard to retain the coercive pattern and suppressed the first revival impulse as quickly as possible. But it was the turn to mass evangelism in the Second Great Awakening, which saved the Trinitarian Congregational churches from the disastrous effects of the Unitarian split and the end of public support.

Those ministers who experienced the first Great Awakening in their churches were taken by surprise. In the Second Great Awakening, launched by Timothy Dwight of Yale, revivals were planned and a methodology developed. Moreover, missionary societies were founded to carry the word at home and abroad. (Neither foreign missions nor home missions was needed as long as Christians were content to accept a political and geographical definition of the Church.) And, finally, special societies expressing various Christian social concerns—temperance, peace, prison reform, abolition of slavery, protection of children, protection of animals from cruelty, the spread of literacy and education—were founded in large number. The Puritan tradition persisted in the determination to "Christianize" the whole society. Although the basis of membership was shifting to voluntaryism, the first practitioners of mass evangelism in the new country had no intention of abandoning the civilizing function of Christianity, of giving up the dream of America as a Christian nation. And whenever a special crisis was at hand or a yet unsolved problem had to be dealt with, they continued for generations to turn easily to the use of governmental authority to further Protestant religious interests.

Statistics on Church Membership

Nothing is more elusive in church history than honest statistics. In recent years, particularly, the American churches have succumbed to the illusion that mere numbers are proof of "success," and that "success" is auto-suggestive. Thus pastors are frequently afraid to clean the rolls and turn in an honest report because it seems a report of failure. Moreover, some churches in America still use the style of reporting which derives from earlier practices in the world of state churches and establishments. This gives them a numerical superiority which they would not have if they reported only active members. This is notably true of the Roman Catholic Church, which counts all the baptized —even if they have ceased to be communicants by the minimal standard of one confession and one communion per year. But all of the major religious bodies keep a large percentage of "dead wood" on the rolls, and church statistics are considerably less reliable than production figures on corn, wheat, pigs, beef. At that, they are no more deceptive than the figures on church membership in European Christendom, where whole populations are still bracketed in as "Catholic," "Orthodox," "Lutheran," "Reformed"—even under Nazism or Communism!

In earlier years the problem was complicated not by the drive for (statistical) prestige but by simple lack of accurate statistics and lack of communication even within denominations. In fact, the keeping of accurate statistics was a result of Free Church attention to individual memberships. Men like John Wesley and Francis Asbury were meticulous in keeping accurate records, down to the last person in each society. But the general carelessness, natural to the old system of counting the total population of a geographical area, long persisted, and most figures on church membership in earlier generations are at best but estimates and summarized impressions. Nevertheless, the intensive attempts given to the problem by Daniel Dorchester (*The Problem of Religious Progress*, 1881) provide us with a wealth of material and, above all, a fairly sound impression of the way in which church membership has grown through a century and a half of mass evangelism.

The picture is one of striking gains in membership and participation, from the time when the churches began to recover from the collapse of established privilege through to the present day. In fact, the results on the North American mission field make it the most successful missionary effort in the world since the beginning of the nineteenth century. We cannot understand the American religious scene at all until we realize how it has been shaped by a century and a half of mass evangelism, and the principle of voluntary membership which travels with it. Here are the best available statistics on the growth of church membership:

1776	5%
1800	6.9%
1850	15.5%
1900	35.7%
1926	50.+%

From 1926 to 1943–44, church membership increased by 32.8 per cent, while local churches increased only 9.3 per cent in number and the population grew 13.9 per cent. With the census of 1960 we stand at a high tide of successful mass evangelism, with voluntary church membership at nearly 70 per cent and popular identification with the churches even higher.

In contrast with the situation on the Continent, where both intellectuals and proletariat had—until the rise of totalitarianism challenged some Christians to a recovery of discipline and integrity—long since emigrated from the churches, there has never been in America an intelligent and coherent anti-clericalism. Such as we have had in America has been, like that of Europe, in reaction to coercive religion; Ethan Allen, Robert C. Ingersoll, and Charles Erskine Scott Wood are perhaps the most representative examples, and all three were reacting to the crushing weight of New England orthodoxy. Anti-religious movements are the product of persecuting or dissolute establishments. In America the Gospel is more endangered by a soft religiosity than by a hard opposition. The statistical situation is given not only by the vast upsurge of membership on a voluntary basis but by the general good will toward the churches in the population as a whole. In February of 1958 a Census Bureau projection of religious preferences showed 115,000,000 Americans fourteen years of age and older who think of themselves as members of religious organizations; these are 96 per cent of the 119,333,000 citizens in that age group; 79,000,000 think of themselves as Protestants, 30,700,000 think of themselves as Roman Catholics, 8,600,000 think of themselves as Jewish or members of minor religious groups. More significant than the absence of coherent or militant anti-religion is the slippage between the number who actually hold membership and those who think of themselves in that category. One fourth of all adult Americans are friendly to "religion," but fail to maintain the most elementary responsibility toward it.

During the years from the camp meetings of the Cane Ridge Revival (1801) in the West and the Second Great Awakening in Connecticut (c. 1798–1811), to the 1960 census more people joined the Christian Church than ever before in her history. This happened in the U.S.A. and— along with the mass immigrations of Catholics and Jews between the Mexican War and World War II—it is the most important single fact in American church history. More than that, the percentage gain was so rapid as to be paralleled by only three other periods in two thousand years. Most Americans are today "new Christians," first- or second-generation Christians, just as truly as are those of the "Younger Churches" in Africa and Asia. This is quite different from the situation in old Europe, where millions among once Christian peoples—Catholic, Protestant, and Orthodox—have drifted away into unbelief or broken away into anti-Christian ideologies. Ours is not a "post-Christian" era. Our problems are those of newness, the problems in every mission field where freshly converted masses carry over into the church the mores of their unbaptized condition. In West Africa the church educators must then fight to eradicate polygamy and the bride price; in parts of Asia the exposure of unwanted infants or reversion to ideas of transmigration or pantheism must be resisted; in America, nativism and racialism, a vulgar "success" philosophy, and uncertain credal orientations are widespread and must be dealt with.

Mass Evangelism

Foreign missionary and home missionary societies were founded as a result of the early revivals. The American Board of Commissioners for Foreign Missions (f. 1810) was founded as a direct result of the revivals in New England.

Other societies followed, on state, local, and denominational lines. Those who saw the necessity of using new techniques to get the word to the distant races and nations were
also keenly aware of the imperative claims of home missions. And it was the use of the revivals and the missionary
societies which set the New England churches back on their
feet, by which they regained and surpassed the strength
lost to the Unitarians. Similarly, it was revivalism coupled
with home missions by which the people of the southern
and western frontiers were reclaimed for the churches and
on a voluntary basis.

With the shift to mass evangelism, the role of the responsible member was stressed. Those who opposed the methods of revivalism did so in the name of sobriety, family
religion, Christian education, social responsibility. The conservative Calvinists, as well as the liberal wing, disliked the
"enthusiasm" and "emotionalism" by which the revivalists
appealed to the common people to convert and join the
churches. That the proper people of the older settlements
resented and resisted revivalism generally has been attributed to theological issues. The conflict between Edwards
and Charles Chauncey of Boston is frequently discussed at
length in ideational terms. And such discussions always end
unsatisfactorily, for they miss the main point. The defenders of reasonable religion, and they were found in both left
(pre-Unitarian) and right (orthodox Puritan) wings, were
above all people committed to the assumption that sound
and sober religion—like political and public life generally—
should be kept out of the hands of the common people.
Their reaction was like that of their contemporary, the
Duchess of Buckingham, who wrote a friend who encour-
aged the Wesleyan preachers in criticism of their work:

> Their doctrines are most repulsive and strongly tinc-
> tured with impertinence and disrespect towards their
> superiors, in perpetually endeavoring to level all ranks
> and do away with all distinctions. It is monstrous to
> be told that you have a heart as sinful as the common
> wretches that crawl on the earth, and I cannot but

wonder that your ladyship should relish any sentiments so much at variance with high rank and good
breeding.[1]

The Duchess was the natural daughter of James II.

Opposition to revivalism led to much division in the
churches. Whole sections of Presbyterianism resisted the
techniques used and split off in a series of anti-revivalist
churches. Resistance to home missions among the Calvinist
Baptists produced the Anti-Missionary Baptists, a strong
church during the nineteenth century. Among the New
England Congregationalists the resistance to the Awakening and its methods informed those better educated circles
which turned to Unitarianism. New England Unitarianism,
originally a movement to defend simple New Testament religion against hard Calvinist scholasticism, became thereby
a type of Bostonian culture-religion, and lost the restitutionist zeal which bid fair at first to sweep the continent.

The theology which was opposed by both right-wing
champions of the way of the old standing order and left-
wing culture-religionists tended inevitably toward "Arminianism": i.e., appeal to the listener to respond to the divine
initiative, convert, and be healed. The old way had been
that of the conversion of whole peoples and tribes, the new
way was, at the point of decision, individualistic. Graf
Zinzendorf stated the logic of the posture of the preachers
of the Awakening as follows:

> We directly oppose the conversion of heathen na-
> tions to the profession of the Christian religion; and
> likewise the method hitherto made use of in the con-
> version of both Jews and heathens. For if Christian
> princes and divines should go so far as to convert the
> heathen nations to their customs and ways in our days,
> they would thereby do the greatest piece of service to
> the Devil.
>
> And I believe concerning those quick and wonder-
> ful conversions of whole nations, where all sorts of peo-

[1] Quoted in Belden, Albert D., *George Whitefield—The
Awakener* (Nashville: Cokesbury Press, 1930), p. 62.

ple good and bad are made Christians, 'tis much the same whether one calls it the work of the LORD or the work of the Devil.

Therefore, it is most plain to us that the conversion of the heathen must be of the same kind as the conversion among those that are already called Christians. And that all the souls among the heathen whom we should admit to baptism, must be awakened to eternal life by the Lord Jesus and his Spirit in like manner as a person in Christendom who would be converted must first be awakened. And therefore have we, in the conversion of the heathen, entirely respected the method of teaching them such matters as they can keep in their head, and learn by rote, to say after one. And a heathen by our way of preaching or instruction in heavenly things, shall not be able so much as to walk when he has not the matter in his heart.

Therefore it is impossible that we can convert the heathen by the thousands; yea 'tis even a wonder to ourselves when we convert them by twentys and thirtys.[2]

Later, the emphasis upon mass conversions—accompanied by a watering down of membership training and standards —was to lead to an infatuation with statistics quite different in consequence from the early revivalists' retention of the classical Christian sequence of conviction of sin, repentance, conversion, acceptance of divine grace, and the gifts of the spirit.

The Breakup of the New England Standing Order

When Isaac Backus presented the cause of the Baptists before the Continental Congress in Philadelphia in 1774, John Adams commented "that one might as well expect a

---

[2] Mode, P. G., ed., *Sourcebook and Bibliographical Guide for American Church History* (Menosha, Wis.: George Banta Publishing Co., 1921), pp. 535–36.

change in the solar system as that the great Puritan Commonwealth would abolish its ecclesiastical laws," and Samuel Adams inferred that the complaints came from enthusiasts who made it a merit to suffer persecution.[3]

While to the South independence brought immediate emancipation from the Anglican establishment, the Massachusetts Convention of 1779 reaffirmed religion as state business. The Commonwealth was slowly and reluctantly moving toward religious freedom, but pressures from outside accomplished finally what the leaders of Christendom could not bring themselves to do voluntarily. It was the coming of Irish Catholic labor into the rising industrial sections which finally forced the issue,[4] but the split of the Trinitarian and Unitarian Congregationalists a few years before had broken the will to maintain a coerced uniformity.

In condemning the prevailing climate of culture-religion the early revivalists were apt to let themselves go. Gilbert Tennent said that "the greatest part by far of the Ministers in this land, were carnal unconverted Men, and that they held damnable *Arminian* Principles" (Boston, 1743). George Whitefield called the Boston ministers "dumb dogs, half devils and half beasts, unconverted, spiritually blind, and leading their people to hell." At the time of the Great Awakening, when these sentiments were uttered, the standing order was intact enough for ministers and public officials to combine and freeze revivalism out. Various pamphlets were published condemning the "uncharitable censorious spirit" of James Davenport, asserting that Whitefield's preaching had "a tendency to promote a spirit of bitterness," and denouncing even the great Jonathan Edwards for dangerous experimentalism. The first Awakening, rather quickly suppressed in the New England parishes, went on to a continuing harvest in the middle and southern colonies. Those little groups in New England which fol-

[3] Burrage, Henry S., "The Contest for Religious Liberty in Massachusetts," VI *Papers of the American Society of Church History* (1893) 156.

[4] Thorning, Joseph Francis, *Religious Liberty in Transition* (Washington, D.C.: Catholic University Press, 1931). Passim.

lowed stubbornly the logic of revivalism and voluntaryism split off and formed Baptist congregations.

The liquidation of the New England standing order or—rather more accurately—its breakup in New England, resulted primarily from two forces:

1. the split between Trinitarian and Unitarian Congregationalists;

2. the immigration of large numbers of poor laborers, chiefly Irish Catholic, to do the heavy work in the cities and factories, and the controlling elements' inability to keep them politically ineffective.

Unitarianism was one of three major parties to emerge in New England Congregationalism at the opening of the nineteenth century, and its leaders were opposed to the other two—the revivalists, the scholastics—just as these were opposed to each other. Originally, Massachusetts Bay Colony had been the chief bulwark of orthodoxy. As a result of the Second Great Awakening, however, and the close association developed in Connecticut between the Congregational churches, by the end of the eighteenth century that state was the main center of vigorous orthodoxy. The leaders of the Connecticut churches gradually learned to combine revivalism, mass evangelism, home missions, and orthodoxy, and when church and state were separated they were equipped to appeal to the common folk for convinced voluntary membership and support. The Connecticut churches suffered no losses to Unitarianism when the split came.

In Massachusetts, however, the churches had been but loosely related to each other. From the time John Wise (1652–1725) wrote his defense of democratic church order against Cotton Mather's plan for a tighter inter-church organization, the Massachusetts churches had remained relatively autonomous. Nor had discipline held up well within the individual parish. Strict standards were progressively abandoned from 1662 on, when the "Half-Way Covenant" was approved by the Boston General Synod. By this, children of parents who could not profess a personal experience of religion were admitted to baptism. Strict covenanters were forced to submit or form new congregations—which a number did, the most famous being the founders of New Ark, New Jersey. In 1700 the unregenerate were admitted to the communion tables with those converted and gathered. In the previous year, Harvard liberals had organized the Brattle Street Church, without consulting the magistrates or neighboring churches and with loosened rules. Moreover, they called as their first minister Benjamin Coleman, a man not ordained by the elders of New England but by the Presbytery of London. In 1701 Increase Mather retired from the presidency of Harvard to work in Second Church of Boston, where his son Cotton Mather assisted him. He had already come to the painful conclusion

It is the judgment of very learned men that, in the glorious times promised to the church on earth, America will be hell.[5]

The standing order in Massachusetts began the eighteenth century with loosened discipline. During the time when the awakenings revitalized the churches of the Connecticut Valley and reached far into former Anglican territory in the South, many parishes in Massachusetts resisted "enthusiasm" bitterly. And it was finally the incoherence between congregation and parish which destroyed the theocracy. Without a strong association between covenanting congregations, the churches were compelled to lean upon the legislature for coherence; and property control and final decision rested with the parishes, not the covenanted congregations within them. By the end of the eighteenth century the parishes in and around Boston were thoroughly liberalized, with the exception of Old South. When Jedidiah Morse was called to the church in Charlestown, Massachusetts, in 1789 it was already too late to save the cause of orthodoxy in that area.

The tensions increased steadily with the rise of home missionary work. In 1787 there was organized the "Congrega-

[5] Quoted in Platner, John W., "The Congregationalists," in *The Religious History of New England* (Cambridge: Harvard University Press, 1917), p. 32.

tional Missionary Society in the Counties of Berkshire (Mass.) and Columbia (N.Y.)." In 1798 the Connecticut Missionary Society was organized and the following year the Massachusetts Missionary Society. In 1802 came the Hampshire Missionary Society, and in 1803 the Massachusetts Society for Promoting Christian Knowledge. In May 1803 the *Massachusetts Missionary Magazine* was launched. After the crucial election of Hollis Ware to the chair of New Testament at Harvard (1805), the Connecticut men ("Hopkinsians") and the old Calvinists in Massachusetts united to found Andover Seminary. Timothy Dwight was invited up to preach the opening sermon. The division between liberal parishes and orthodox churches was rapidly institutionalized, and it was the revivalists who carried the day for orthodoxy—not without being attacked from the conservative side as well as from the liberal, even after they won most of the conservatives to an uneasy union with the home missions and revivalist party.

The Trinitarian Congregationalists, with the men from Yale and the Connecticut Valley giving most of the leadership, rapidly formed one society after another to win voluntary support for the cause which was steadily losing ground in courts and legislatures. Lyman Beecher launched the first Temperance Society in 1812. In 1816 Bangor Seminary (Maine) was established. In the same year was set up the Boston Female Society for the Promotion of Christianity Among the Jews. In 1818 was founded the Domestic Missionary Society of Massachusetts Proper, for meeting the problems attendant on the Unitarian secession. In 1821 Amherst College was founded; after three years of fighting in the legislature that "engine of orthodoxy" was chartered. The American Peace Society, American Sunday School Union, American Tract Society, and finally the American Colonization Society all gained strength and support from the energetic organizing thrust of the Congregationalists. No effort was more significant than the founding of the American Board of Commissioners for Foreign Missions in 1810, a work initiated by students converted at Williams College under the Second Great Awakening. Here, as generally, the back country churches in Massachusetts supported the revivals, even though at the end of the Unitarian secession every parish but one within fifty miles of Boston had been lost to orthodoxy.

From the very beginning the revivals have had the whole man and the whole of society as their target. Indeed, as Timothy Smith has pointed out in *Revivalism and Social Reform* (1957), the major social movements of the nineteenth century were the fruit of the new style of mass evangelism. There was at that time none of the narrow concentration on the world of individual and familial religion, coupled with a hearty affirmation of the dominant culture and spirit of the times, which has characterized a spurious latterday "revivalism." Lyman Beecher (1775–1863), one of the great leaders, surveyed the battle lines and put the case forthrightly:

> Unitarians will gain the victory if we are left without revivals, but they will perish by the breath of His mouth and the brightness of His coming if revivals prevail.[6]

And on another occasion he wrote for discipline and separation:

> All, however, do not receive the truth in the love of it. The church is called to an internal conflict. Its attention must be directed to the dangers which now threaten it. It must be cautioned against abandonment of the faith once delivered to the saints; and must be taught to guard against an amalgamation with the world.[7]

One of the magazines founded during the controversy was a monthly journal called *The Spirit of the Pilgrims.* Few have realized even to this day that it was the failure of the Pilgrims and their allies consistently to live by that

[6] Beecher, Lyman, *Autobiography, Correspondence, etc.* (New York: Harper's, 1866), I, 389.

[7] Quoted in Mead, Sidney, *Nathaniel William Taylor: 1786–1858* (Chicago: Chicago University Press, 1942), p. 53.

spirit which brought disaster to their descendents. For the religious program of a voluntary covenant was unequally yoked, in the state churches founded in Plymouth and the allied settlements, to a parish system which in 1818–20 enabled the Unitarians to carry off large sections of Massachusetts Christendom. In the Dedham Case it was decided that church property was held by the parish and not by the covenanting congregation. The parishes were liberal, and in many cases carried the properties and church buildings out from under the people who actually carried the faith by their prayers and attendance. Thus the Unitarian victory, particularly in the Boston area, was achieved by use of the political controls built into the New England order by the fathers. The Rev. Dr. Enoch Pond, afterwards of Bangor Theological Seminary, said:

> We call the proceedings by the hard name of *plunder*. And we call upon the courts of Massachusetts to revoke these unrighteous decisions and put the Congregational churches of the state upon their original and proper basis.[8]

What he apparently didn't realize was that the reason the Congregational churches lost out was because they were upon their "original" basis!

The nineteenth century opened with anti-Trinitarianism riding high in the new republic. In 1796–1802 the governor of Kentucky was a Unitarian, James Garrard. So also was Harry Toulmin, President of Transylvania Seminary and Secretary of the State of Kentucky. In 1822 Thomas Jefferson said, "I trust that there is not a *young man* now living in the United States who will not die an Unitarian." Earlier, John C. Calhoun had observed that Unitarianism would be the religion of the country in fifty years.[9] Moreover, the

[8]*Unitarianism: its Origin and History* (Boston: 1890), p. 148 n; edited by H. G. Spaulding from sixteen lectures delivered at Channing House.

[9] Gohdes, Clarence, "Some Notes on the Unitarian Church in the Ante-Bellum South . . . ," in Jackson, David K., ed., *American Studies in Honor of Wm. K. Boyd* (Durham, N.C.: Duke University Press, 1942), p. 327.

period of Jared Sparks's Baltimore Sermon (1819) and the founding of the American Unitarian Association (1825) saw the emergence on the western frontier of one of the most vigorous anti-Trinitarian movements in history: the "Disciples" or "Christians."

New England Unitarianism began as an anti-speculative movement and there were many who opposed the forming of an association because they didn't want to be known as a separate sectarian movement with a separate name. In opposition to Calvinist scholasticism, they stressed a simple gospel without glosses. The first Unitarian church in Baltimore was called "First Independent Christian Church." And in 1841 when James Freeman Clarke founded a church in Boston it took the name, "Church of the Disciples in Boston."

Restitutionism on the Frontier

In the start of the movements led by Alexander Campbell (1788–1866) and Barton W. Stone on the American frontier, the restitution of primitive Christian unity also played a vital role. For years the new movement sought fellowship with the Presbyterians and the Baptists and welcomed into the groups of "Christians" and "Disciples" all who sought a return to the original foundation and practice of the early church. Alexander Campbell's father, Thomas, authored an historic *Declaration and Address* (1809) which became the platform of a movement which now counts two of the largest religious groupings in the U.S.A. —the Churches of Christ and the Disciples of Christ. In the *Declaration*, the points stated launched the "Restorationist Movement." Among them were these: the Church of Christ has essential unity; sectarian divisions among Christians are un-Christian; the cure for such divisions is the restoration of the New Testament church.

As the movement gained momentum, Alexander Campbell founded *The Millennial Harbinger*, a widely circulated church paper (1830–68), and Bethany College (f. 1840), still a fine Christian institution. Studying the New Testament, Campbell and his colleagues settled upon a program in which the standards of the Early Church were to be followed at all points: Simon Peter's confession of faith; believers' baptism; congregational form of government; observance of weekly communion, with the simple words of institution. Christian reunion was to be achieved by reducing theological and institutional and liturgical discipline to the essential minimum. Again, the reductionist approach to such matters is a perennial characteristic of restitutionist groups.

Unitarianism: A Permanent Minority

The Disciples of Christians refused to enforce the trinitarian formula as a test of orthodoxy, and for a time it seemed the two anti-speculative movements might combine forces. With the Unitarians in control of the major university and chief cultural enterprises in the east, and the Disciples winning their way in the west, the Republic might in fact have become Unitarian. But it was an uneven alliance, never truly realized. The reasons, primarily nontheological, can be readily summarized:

1. The Disciples were revivalists, and built their voluntary congregations of common folk;

2. The Unitarians made their chief gains at the first, by using the state-church controls and parish system;

3. The Unitarians centered in Harvard and in Boston, and remained centered intellectually in eastern cultural circles and their literary and philosophical interests;

4. In the second generation, the Unitarian leaders shifted from an anti-speculative stance to a base in German idealistic philosophy. The Unitarians were drawn up in the activities of the "Hedge Club," a brilliant circle of speculative thinkers including James Freeman Clarke, A. Bronson Alcott, Margaret Fuller, Elizabeth Peabody, and Theodore Parker. The leader was Ralph Waldo Emerson, who resigned his pastorate in 1832 and in 1838 delivered his fa-

mous "Divinity School Address." The Transcendentalists
developed a veritable passion for the new things of the German philosophy. With Alcott it was Plotinus; with Margaret Fuller, Plato and the Greek legends; with Emerson,
the Hindu and Persian mystics; with George Ripley, Schlei-
ermacher and the later French Utopian Socialist leaders;
with Theodore Parker, De Wette and biblical criticism. We
might include also O. B. Frothingham's spread of the results of the Tübingen school's criticism (F. C. Baur). But
the man of the frontier was far more responsive to experimental religion and revivalism than to the "turning of the
red slayer" or *The Select Journal of Foreign Literature*
(f. 1833).

5. Finally, the fatal weakness of Unitarianism was its lack
of missionary activity, which was considered incompatible
with their views of the dignity of man.

The Unitarian abdication of national religious leadership
was summarized by Theodore Parker himself shortly before he died:

> No sect had ever a finer opportunity than the Uni-
> tarians to advance the religious development of a peo-
> ple. But they let it slide, and now they must slide with
> it. In 1838 the Unitarians were the controlling party in
> Boston: the railroads were just getting opened and it
> was plain the Protestant population of the town would
> soon double. Young men with no fortune but their
> character would come in from the country and settle
> and grow rich; the Unitarians ought to have welcomed
> such to their churches; to have provided helps for them
> and secured them to the Unitarian fold. Common pol-
> icy would suggest that course not less than a refined
> humanity. But they did no such thing: they loved
> pecunia pecuniata, not pecunia pecunians. They were
> aristocrats and exclusive in their tastes, not democratic
> and inclusive. So they shoved off these young country
> fellows, and now rejoice in their very respectable and
> very little congregations. The South of Boston is not in

the Unitarian churches. A church of old men goes to its grave, one of young men goes to its work.[10]

When Lewis Tappan, one of the most prominent of abolitionist Unitarians, resigned from that connection in 1828 he wrote:

> For some years I have seen, that the Unitarian denomination did not give equal evidence with the orthodox of their spirituality and liberal giving. I have been persuaded, from my own observation, that they did not, in an equal degree, consider themselves as stewards, and their property as consecrated to the cause of Christianity; and that they were greatly deficient in a devotional frame of mind.

He found himself forced back to the orthodox movement by the thought that "by their fruits ye shall know them." He contrasted the spirit shown by the American Unitarian Association with that of the American Board of Commissioners, and praised the latter for its lack of divisive speculation and its earnest piety.[11]

The Revival Churches

Thus, at the time the Disciples, Methodists, and Baptists were coming to the fore in the launching of a series of great revivals, and even the New England orthodox were shifting to a new style of home missions and voluntaryism, the Unitarians settled back into the status of a permanent and tiny minority. They were yet to give several Presidents and other public leaders to the American Republic, but they never again were to have an opportunity such as they missed at the beginning of the nineteenth century.

[10] Quoted in Fenn, Wm. W., "The Revolt Against the Standing Order," in *The Religious History of New England*, op. cit., p. 112.

[11] Tappan, Lewis, *Letter from a Gentleman in Boston to a Unitarian Clergyman of that City* (Boston: T. R. Marvin, 1828), 2d edition, p. 6.

It was mass evangelism and the style of church life that it produced that made voluntaryism a permanent part of religion in America. The common interpretation is that voluntary support dates from the separation of church and state at the beginning of the Republic. In fact, however, the churches accustomed themselves but slowly and reluctantly to the prospect of voluntary support of religious education and church life. Again and again, confronted by special problems or opportunities, they reverted to the old custom of using government or tax monies to support church work. It was the revivals, however, that made voluntaryism a possibility. They brought the laity alive and produced a sympathetic co-operation of clergy and laity such as the best of the establishment rarely saw.[12]

In the East and even across the Alleghenies the churches used tax monies for schools, colleges, care of Indians and freedmen, chaplaincies in public institutions, etc. In the valleys of the Ohio and Mississippi, where voluntary support came into its own, it was the central place held by camp meetings and revivalistic techniques that made voluntary giving and support a practical possibility. The very founding of churches, once the old centers of transplanted European Christendom were left behind, depended upon the winning of members afresh through home missions and the organizing of support and discipline on a strictly voluntary basis. Unfortunately, the anxiety of the American churches —deriving chiefly from "the Left Wing of the Reformation" —has led them to stress their tie to the sixteenth century Reformers and depreciate the unique aspects of the American setting. More than that, there has been insufficient appreciation of the fact that for half of American history establishments of the European type dominated the scene and that religious voluntaryism and pluralism is a comparatively new thing even in America. The romantic myth about separation of church and state and the "Founding

[12] Bolles, James Aaron, *The Revival System* (Cleveland: Pinkerton and Nevins, 1858), pp. 5–16.

Fathers" has served simply to confuse thinking about the issue.

For, in spite of the statistical evidence to the contrary, the myth of America as a "Christian nation" (Protestant) continued and was, strangely enough, part of the revivalists' repertoire as well. Faced by the collapse of the colonial state churches and the exit of most of the population from the churches altogether, the revivalists did not in their home missions efforts address themselves in the language of missionaries in a heathen land—which in fact they were. They held high the memory of the Pilgrim Fathers and those colonists who first came for religious reasons, ignoring the economic factors which had in fact motivated most immigrants, and creating thereby the most persistent myth of American history: that the "Founding Fathers" of the colonies came to found religious liberty and that the "Founding Fathers" of the Republic were above all dedicated to the cause of liberty. Today, with the non-historical mentality what it is, the myths of the two sets of "Founding Fathers" are telescoped into one and the image of the good old days is a fixed point in Protestant nativist circles and in reactionary thinking generally.

In his *Commentaries on the Constitution*, Mr. Justice Story referred to the United States as a Protestant nation and declared that Christianity was part of the common law. His commentaries, first published in 1833 and going through many editions, supplied the lawyers and other literates with the same notion of American religious history as the revivalists planted in the mind of the common people. Mr. Justice Story, one of the ten most important personalities in American legal history, was a Massachusetts man. The facts are far different: with the collapse of the colonial state churches America became visibly what it had in fact been even during the pretension of the New England theocracy and Anglican establishments—a heathen people.

During the major part of the nineteenth century, America was missionary territory. But the Americans continued to see themselves not as they were, a needy missionary field, but as a part of European Christendom. This image continues to the present day, confusing our teaching of church history in the seminaries, darkening counsel as to the nature of the problems confronting American churches. The American churches are today the "bright morning star" of the Younger Churches, those churches created by the Great Century of Christian Missions. They belong in theology, ethics, and morals, and in ordinary organizational problems, to the "Younger Churches" rather than to "Christendom" in the old and coercive sense. It is only within this generation that a few theologians and church historians have begun to see and interpret the true facts of the case: that the churches of the U.S.A., instead of being a part of the general collapse of Christendom in Europe (the "post-Christian era"), are in fact the first fruits of mass evangelism and Christian missions. There are two factors which have created modern religious life in America: 1) a century and a half of mass evangelism during which the pattern and style of voluntaryism shaped Protestantism; and 2) a century of immigrations, Roman Catholic and Jewish, which created a pluralistic situation, with citizens of these traditions entitled by law to the same recognition and consideration as those of the older and predominantly Protestant immigrations.

Voluntaryism and pluralism complement each other, but the recognition of that fact—and the development of a Protestant approach to public life appropriate to it—requires the destruction of the myth of the "Founding Fathers."

Although it was revivalism which redeemed America from open heathenism, opposition to mass evangelism was vocal from the start. The use of revivalist measures did not go without challenge even in the decades when camp meetings and public revivals were almost the only methods for taking the Christian message to the masses of unchurched people. An Episcopal clergyman, Bernard Whitman, published a representative statement of the objections of the cultured and educated to such common methods of influencing the impressionable as "whispering meetings" and "inquiry meetings." The former were said to be largely attended by women, and Mr. Whitman described the procedures:

> Either the minister or some male assistant passes around the room and whispers something into the ear of every individual. He generally repeats some striking passage of scripture, or gives some solemn admonition, or utters some awakening truth, or puts some startling question, or pronounces some unauthorized assertion. By the stillness and deathlike silence of the scene; by the ghastly appearance of every countenance on which the dying light casts its paleness; by a sudden change in the train of thought or state of feeling, he hopes to excite a high degree of terror and agitation. For when the timid subject is thoroughly frightened, she can be molded at pleasure; she can be induced to make any acknowledgements, and sign any confessions and give her consent to any creed and adopt any party measure.[13]

Of the "meetings of inquiry" he was equally critical, although these had played a significant role in the development of the Second Great Awakening under the leadership of such sober ministers as Timothy Dwight and Lyman Beecher and had been fundamental in the development of home and foreign missions societies. He wrote bitterly:

> When the unconverted have become so much terrified, as to confess themselves totally depraved, haters of their heavenly Father and enemies of all goodness, they assemble on the appointed evening to inquire either of the minister or some church member what they must do to be saved. None are admitted but those who feel anxious for the salvation of their souls. . . . No discussion of disputed questions is allowed. . . .[14]

This is a caricature of mass evangelism of course. More than that, it is the natural reaction of a sophisticated clergy-

[13] Whitman, Bernard, *Letter to An Orthodox Minister on Revivals of Religion* (Boston: Gray and Bowen, 1831), p. 17.
[14] Ibid., p. 18.

man to the sweaty and naive spiritual wrestlings of simple folk. Most of all, it is the attitude taken by all of the leaders of the establishments—Unitarian, Congregationalist, Anglican, Orthodox Presbyterian, Confessional Lutheran—who believed that religion should be handled with sobriety and in due form by those trained to keep it from getting out of hand.

Nevertheless, by the middle of the century it was the revival churches which predominated and put their impress upon public life. Although Catholics and Jews were beginning to come in some numbers, the real floodtide of their immigration was not reached until after the Civil War. Those that came previously lived chiefly in ghettos within a society that they thought of, and that thought of itself, as Protestant. The Protestant Episcopal Church had begun to recover, and had attained some status among the privileged classes of the East. Lutherans had arrived in some numbers, including a powerful immigration of intransigents who had resisted the enforcement of the Prussian Union of 1817, but they too kept largely to themselves. The churches before the public eye, who followed the people westward from frontier to frontier, who conducted the great revivals in the eastern cities and camp meetings in the West, were the Methodists, Baptists, Disciples, and the missionary Congregationalists and Presbyterians.

The fateful linking of revivalism with various moral crusades, which was the genius of radical Protestantism, was not without its drawbacks. Characteristic of the problem was the progressive abandonment of church discipline, coupled with the tendency to revert to political legislation to handle what had once been matters of rules of conduct. The success of mass evangelism, which has demonstrated itself in geometric proportion for a century and a half, was accompanied by a steady deterioration of the standards of membership. Here, too, the logic of the home missions approach conflicted with the image of America as a Christian nation. The gospel message was "repent, change, and be healed." The reconciling Word in Christ Jesus was that all the broken and corrupted creation should be restored to

God's purpose for it. And sometimes the great revivalists proclaimed this Word with power. On the other hand, even the revivalists clung—most of them—to the romantic notion that America had been founded as a Christian (Protestant) nation, that the Founding Fathers were men of deep religious devotion, that America's greatest need was to return to a previous condition of virtue and religious rectitude. Hence the harsh word of repentance and conversion and discontinuity was progressively muted, as it was discovered that larger masses of people would join the churches to affirm a traditional view of America than would actually join by conversion and change of life. It was the Civil War and the propaganda on both sides, as well as the acute problems which arose out of it, which virtually eliminated church discipline and internal integrity in the larger Protestant bodies and fixed the revivalist churches in a hearty affirmation of "the American way of life" or "the southern way of life."

As the nineteenth century opened, and the church memberships were but a tiny minority of the population, the churches maintained some requirements for admission to membership and some standards for retention of it. The Puritan covenants had been strongly ethical as well as theological, and during the first revivals a reform of life was required as well as a clear profession of experiential religion. "Owning the Covenant" was then no empty phrase. On the frontier, the church courts frequently served as the major civilizing and disciplinary force amidst a semiliterate and half-barbarous population. The Methodist class meeting, which retained some strength up to the mid-century mark, may be taken as an example of a disciplinary instrument.

The Problem of Church Discipline

The revival churches were all restitutionist in their view of church polity, seeking to restore those New Testament ordinances which had obtained in the Christian church before the "Fall of the Church." Church discipline was char-

acteristically based on a certain reading of the life of the
Early Church. From 1786 on the Methodist *Discipline* provided a rule of discipline for membership:

> But in cases of neglect of duties of any kind, im-
> prudent conduct, indulging sinful tempers or words,
> disobedience to the order and discipline of the church.
> First, let the private reproof be given by a leader or
> preacher; if there be an acknowledgement of the fault
> and proper humiliation, the person may remain on
> trial. On a second offence, a preacher may take one or
> two faithful friends. On a third failure, if the transgres-
> sion be increased or continued, let it be brought be-
> for the society, or a select number: if there be no sign
> of humiliation, and the church is dishonored, the of-
> fender must be cut off.

Drunkenness, fornication, light living, dishonesty in business, "disorderly walking," etc., were among the grounds
for rebuke and—if not corrected—expulsion. The Methodist
people were expected to live according to the Kingdom and
not according to the world, and in many places they were
known for their simple dress and uprightness of life.

Nor was the discipline primarily negative, although up-
holding it might require an occasional expulsion. No one
was to be admitted in the first place who could not profess
an inward change and desire to put on the new man. This
brought the charge of sectarianism and enthusiasm from the
defenders of the old order. In England John Wesley an-
swered similar charges as follows:

> Our twentieth Article defines a true Church, "a con-
> gregation of faithful people, wherein the true word of
> God is preached and the sacraments duly adminis-
> tered." According to this account the Church of Eng-
> land is that body of faithful people (or holy believers)
> in England among whom the pure word of God is
> preached and the sacraments duly administered. Who,
> then, are the worst Dissenters from this Church? (1)
> Unholy men of all kinds; swearers, Sabbath-breakers,

drunkards, fighters, whore-mongers, liars, revilers, evil-speakers; the passionate, the gay, the lovers of money, the lovers of dress or of praise, the lovers of pleasure more than the lovers of God: all these are Dissenters of the highest sort, continually striking at the root of the Church, and themselves in truth belonging to no Church, but to the synagogue of Satan. (2) Men unsound in the faith; those who deny the Scriptures of truth, those who deny the Lord that brought them, those who deny justification by faith alone, or the present salvation which is by faith: these also are Dissenters of a very high kind; for they likewise strike at the foundation, and, were their principles universally to obtain, there could be no true Church upon earth. Lastly, those who unduly administer the sacraments; who (to instance but in one point) administer the Lord's Supper to such as have neither the power nor the form of godliness. These, too, are gross Dissenters from the Church of England, and should not cast the first stone at others.[15]

On the American frontier the Methodists also claimed to represent the true and apostolic faith and to have a New Testament church order in their societies, and rebuked those who longed for the old colonial state churches. When had the Methodists "ever been accused of *burning* their enemies"? When had they "*ever made laws compelling others to support* them"?[16] They were frankly free churchmen, and part of their churchmanship was the maintenance of a standard of internal discipline to honor the Lord of the Church.

John Wesley's founding of the class meeting as a means of grace and instrument of instruction was a result of his own wise scepticism toward mere numerical success. As John S. Simon put it in his *Manual of Instruction and Advice for Class Leaders* (1893),

[15] Cameron, Richard M., *The Rise of Methodism: A Source Book* (New York: Philosophical Library, 1954), p. 291.
[16] Quoted in Clark, Robert D., *The Life of Matthew Simpson* (New York: Macmillan Co., 1956), p. 51.

John Wesley, whose clear eyes were never dazzled by mere numerical success, watched the swift increase of his Societies with a joy that was tempered by caution. He saw that he was becoming embarrassed by the rapid multiplication of new centres, and by the ingathering of multitudes of comparatively unknown converts. It was borne in upon him that an exact and individual supervision of such persons was essential.[17]

In the Wesleyan Methodist Conference of England and the Methodist Episcopal Church of Germany the class meeting still exists; in America, however, it hardly outlasted the Civil War. It was in this period that the divided Methodist movement, the largest of all Protestant communions, identified itself enthusiastically and uncritically with the political and cultural interests of each side of the struggle.

It must be emphasized that the low level of Christian life, so far as the common people were concerned, was a fruit of formal state churchism during the colonial period as well as the natural loosening of social controls on the frontier. As William Warren Sweet put it,

> Throughout the entire colonial period, at least until the colonial awakenings, the great mass of the lower classes were little influenced by organized religion; and only a very small proportion of the total population of the thirteen colonies were members of the colonial churches. At the end of the colonial period there were undoubtedly more unchurched people in North America, in proportion to the population, than were to be found in any other land in Christendom.

Sweet went on to describe the situation of the embattled churches:

> That every frontier was in pressing need of moral restraint and guidance there can be no reasonable doubt, and in most instances the only guardians of the

[17] Simon, John O., *A Manual of Instruction and Advice for Class Leaders* (London: Charles H. Kelly, 1893), pp. 2–3.

morale of these communities were the little frontier churches.

On every frontier from the Alleghenies to the Pacific these were the people who fought the battle for decency and order, and to a large degree saved the west from semi-barbarism, and the attitudes created by these bitter struggles remain to this day.[18]

By mid-century, however, a professor at Oxford, Georgia, was lamenting the decline of the disciplinary groups and concluding

It is, therefore, an imperfect discharge of ministerial duty, a misguided defective church policy, a worldly element of pride and self-sufficiency in the membership, and not any new light which the history of the Church has thrown upon the character of class meetings as an element of church economy, that have depreciated their position in the operation of Methodism.[19]

The truth is that the emphasis on discipline became more and more involved with the controversy on slaveholding, and after the Civil War the white churches no longer had the inclination to stress the principle of discontinuity which made discipline meaningful, indeed possible at all. Revivalism, through Charles G. Finney and other great preachers, became identified with abolitionism. And among the northern revival churches the discipline against slaveholding gradually took precedent over every other ethical issue. It divided the major churches, with the exception of the Catholic and Episcopal, and their division prepared the way for the political and military conflict to come.

Abolitionism too was a Puritan crusade, and during the first decades of the movement the Colonization Societies sprang up in the centers of radical Protestantism. In the

[18] Sweet, William Warren, "The Churches as Moral Courts of the Frontier," II *Church History* (1933) 1:3–22, 3, 10, 21.

[19] Sasnett, W. J., "Theory of Methodist Class Meetings," V *The Methodist Quarterly Review* (South) (1851) 2:265–84, 283.

first period of the anti-slavery movement two thirds of all the societies were lodged in Methodist and Baptist churches. At this stage there were many societies south of the Mason-Dixon line as well as in New England and the East. The conclusive stage of the anti-slavery movement was reached when the emphasis on colonization, whose most notable achievement was the founding of Liberia as a settlement of freedmen, yielded to that of abolitionism. Here two new forces entered the picture: 1) the alliance of abolitionism with revivalism, and 2) the growth of "free soil" political action in the Midwest.

In its final stages, radical abolitionism derived its main support in the great farming areas of Ohio, Illinois, Wisconsin, Iowa, and the other new states of the upper Mississippi Valley. Here Lyman Beecher taught the message of conversion and vital religion as seminary head (Lane Theological Seminary) and saw his ablest students walk out to join the new center of abolition and Puritan perfectionism at Oberlin. Oberlin was not only a chief center of revivalism in the West: it was the first college accepting both men and women, whites and Negroes, on equal terms. Here in the West the Republican Party was founded and carried the presidential election of 1860 behind that perfect symbol of free rural America, Abraham Lincoln. From this area came the farm boys who, after "Yankees" and "Southern Gentlemen" had fought two years of inconclusive Civil War, gave General U. S. Grant the slogging and bloody victories which crushed the Confederacy. As the Battle of Gettysburg (July 1–4, 1863) marked the high tide of the Confederate advance, the Battle of Chattanooga (November 23–25, 1863) in the West signaled the beginning of the end for the Southern cause.

The Spread of the New England Way

According to common interpretation, the New England standing order came to an end in the generation following the Revolution. Actually, the traditional style of sustaining and controlling social life and mores continued in two sig-

nificant directions. On the one hand, the Unitarian movement represented an effort to maintain the goals of Christendom, of a continuum of Christ and culture. This tradition
the Unitarians still carry on, although more recently a considerable section has identified itself almost completely with
the spirit of the times (humanism and secularism).

There was a second direction in which the New England
tradition of social, cultural, and religious affairs carried
over, and that was in a scattering of Christian communities
across the tier of northern states out into the Mississippi
Valley. Protest emigrations began early, as the standing order began to lose its grip. Many fled westward, of course,
to seek the freedom of the frontier. Various historians, notably Walter Prescott Webb, have shown the way in which
the frontier served as a solvent of the old coercive social
and political structures—in the original colonies as well as
in Europe.

> . . . Democracy is a frontier institution so far as the
> modern world is concerned.[20]

Both indentured servitude and colonial state churches
could not outlast the original thirteen colonies. America was
early filled in part by refugees from the wars of religion,
just as later by those who escaped the savage pogroms of
the czars.

> It is very significant that for 150 years during which
> the foundations of frontier societies were being laid
> down in the Americas the prevailing condition in the
> Metropolis was that of religious wars and unprece-
> dented intolerance.[21]

But it is a mistake, and a frequent one, to assume that
those who fled westward from oppression were devoted to
a philosophical principle of "freedom." What most sought
was the liberty to live according to their convictions, and
these convictions often led them to establish variant forms

[20] Webb, Walter Prescott, *The Great Frontier* (Boston:
Houghton Mifflin Co., 1942), p. 30.
[21] Ibid., p. 89.

of Christendom even more coercive and intolerant of non-conformity than they or their fathers had themselves suffered.

Thus, from an early date, we find family groups and sometimes whole congregations moving westward to set up Christian communities on the pattern which was losing out in the East. New Haven and New Ark were among the first which were founded to enforce a style of Christendom which was slackening in the original settlements. And, particularly during the first half of the nineteenth century, New England groups moved westward. Some sought freedom in the West; just as many sought to reclaim a lost intactness of religion and politics. Others, in the chaos of semibarbarous life on the frontier, naturally reverted so far as possible to the way of doing things which they understood.

Long after the Puritan oligarchy had lost out in the East, it was possible—right up to the time extreme mobility and the high pace of industrialism changed the whole style of American civilization—to find towns and rural areas in Ohio, Indiana, Illinois, Iowa, the Dakotas, Nebraska, Kansas, etc., where New England culture-religion survived intact. In these Puritan communities the Protestant clergy still played a strong and sometimes controlling role in politics; the churches dominated the cultural, moral, and educational life of the villages or townships. The New England standing order did not break up suddenly: it has survived in scattered areas right into the twentieth century. Much of the anti-Catholicism, anti-Semitism, anti-refugee sentiment, racialism, and nativism which mark the Protestant underworld today derives its support from islands of defensive culture-religion which resent being passed by in the flow of national history. In a degenerate and negative way they live with eyes cast backward, as unworthy of the fathers who once stormed a continent as they are of the present hour.

The colonization process referred to was carried through spontaneously by dozens of groups who seeded the Puritan style of Christendom in cultural islands across the country

while much of the main thrust went into service organizations. The civic initiative and genius of organization for
social good which characterized Puritanism at its best can
be studied better today in Kiwanis, Rotary, the Optimists,
the Lions, than in Winesburg, Ohio, or Keokuk, Iowa.
These groups are the flowering of Puritanism just as the
small towns on the old "Bible Belt" were its fossils. But there
were also many communities established with more strict
regimen yet. When we turn the pages of nineteenth-century
America, toward which many self-styled champions of
Protestant Americanism and "private initiative" look, we are
astonished at the large number of self-contained Christian
communities established—disciplined not only in religion but
in total economy as well.

Considerable attention has been given by historians and
sociologists to the Utopian Socialist colonies which were
founded in that period (Fourier phalanxes, New Harmony,
Icarias and others), and also to the Pietist colonies which
were far more successful (Economy and Harmony, Amana,
Bethel and Aurora, etc.). These were not as different as
often thought today, when another type of socialism has
come to the fore: men like Etienne Cabet thought of their
economic experiments as "true Christianity." And the New
Englanders had their Brook Farm and Hopedale. Like the
German Pietists, they idealized the Church at Jerusalem,
where all they that believed held their property in common.
But equally important in the founding of such colonies was
the impulse of Puritanism. The survival of the New England
order in pockets across the country was also represented by
perfectionist communities such as Oneida, the peculiar
colony founded and led by the visionary Congregational
preacher, John Humphrey Noyes.

The abolitionist crusade, especially, marked the high
tide of Puritan influence in American public life, although
the large Protestant churches continued to attempt the legislation of public morality. In this they were more successful
in states, counties, and cities where they were dominant
than in the national scene. Nevertheless, the Midwest and
East continued "safely Republican" long after massive im-

migrations of Roman Catholics, Jews, and Eastern Orthodox had in fact changed the religious and cultural structure of American society. By resisting the redistricting of state legislative bodies to provide fair representation for the mushrooming metropolitan areas, American Protestantism—based in village and rural life—was able up to the Great Depression and World War II to maintain a power structure which fitted the old image of Protestant America. According to this image America had been founded as a Christian nation, and this myth was repeated with approval and increasing vehemence as the facts mounted which belied the statement.

New England did not "die" with the end of the establishments: it scattered out across the land, hurling its seed as far as Utah, the West Coast, and the Hawaiian Islands. Thus it came about that, long after the "second" and "third" colonization of New England buried all but the most sturdy fortresses of the old order in an avalanche of Irish and Italian immigrants, little fragments of New England society persisted in Indiana, Iowa, Kansas, etc., through to the social upheavals and population mobility which began in the 1930s. What H. L. Mencken resented and repudiated in "Keokuk, Iowa," was the same stark righteousness and unflagging industry, aesthetic barrenness, and latent intolerance which earlier critics had found so unattractive in New England Christendom. It cannot be denied that a combined revivalism and Puritanism performed a major service in civilizing and subduing the frontier settlements. But again the two thrusts in American Protestantism remained unresolved—on the one hand the missionary and evangelical drive toward voluntaryism and internal discipline, and on the other hand the continuing tendency to revert to government and law to enforce church judgments and positions.

It can be seen how this worked out in the abandonment of internal discipline in the pre-Civil War period, accompanied by the growing identification of religious mores with those prevailing in the society at large. Initially, almost all were agreed that slaveholding was unsuitable for Christians. Oglethorpe forbade it in Georgia. The founding Conference of the Methodist Episcopal Church ruled against it. The Baptists maintained mixed Negro and white congregations until after the Revolution. Only the Quakers, among those directly affected, proceeded consistently along classical Free Church lines. From 1688 to 1774, under the impress of such men as John Woolman (1720–72), the societies "talked up" the matter of slaveholding, and finally came to the conclusion that it was incompatible with the profession of Christian faith. They then turned to fellow citizens, backed by the integrity of their own disciplined witness, and urged abolition of the slave trade and slaveholding. Southern Quakers paid a high price for their faithfulness as feelings intensified, moving from their old homes in Virginia and the Carolinas up into Ohio and Indiana in the 1840s and 1850s to be free of a society increasingly committed to maintenance of slavery at all costs. The dominant churches, expanding rapidly, were too impatient to work through the issue in brotherly fashion. They turned almost automatically to legislation as a means of resolving a public issue which they could not even resolve within their own ranks by study and prayer. The coming of the Civil War represented a breakdown of American statesmanship; the mishandling of the issue of slaveholding represented a breakdown in the white churches, too.

When the Civil War broke out both the northern churches and the southern churches claimed to represent Christian civilization, and identified themselves with the spirit of the times and ethos prevailing in their section. The church membership in the country at that time was actually less than 20 per cent of the population.

CHAPTER III

The Civil War and Aftermath

The American Republic plunged into the Civil War with the image of a Christian nation securely fixed in mind. The zealous abolitionists reflected the combination of New England ethical zeal and revivalism, and the apologists for the ante-bellum South read Sir Walter Scott and proof-texted from the Bible to prove that the children of Ham were purposed for slavery from the beginning. Most tragic of all was the breakdown of communication between the sections, a breakdown which started with the divisions in the churches —Methodist, Presbyterian, Baptist, and which created a situation in which the most strenuous efforts were made to suppress discussion altogether. It was the Gag Law passed by the House of Representatives in 1832, a law which tabled without discussion all petitions against slavery, that made the Civil War inevitable. The only alternative, in the final analysis, to violence and coercion in public policy is the maintenance of full, free and informed discussion as the base of legislation.

Division in the Churches

The sectional division of the country which ended in Civil War (1861–65) was preceded by rancor and division in the churches. One of the first schisms occurred in 1837–38 among the Presbyterians. Although the split of New

School and Old School was ostensibly along theological lines, in fact the South remained with the Old School and the alliance of abolitionism and revivalism shaped the New School General Assembly. The Old School intention was stated by Breckenridge of Kentucky:

> He was going to lay no burden on men which neither they nor their fathers were able to bear. . . . Never would he consent that it should be mooted at all, until the church had first got back upon sound and orthodox ground. . . .[1]

In other words, the old line Presbyterians resisted mass revivalism in the name of the traditional covenant theology —and especially for the sake of the place of children in the covenant—and opposed the emphasis on voluntaryism, both organizational and ethical. The southerners joined with the Old School in an effort to suppress discussion of the anti-slavery issue, and the Old School Assembly in fact avoided mention of it until 1861. The revivalists, with Theodore Dwight Weld a powerful influence, were nearly all aboli-tionists. The deal which was made, although carefully disguised and subsequently repeatedly denied, was one in which the Old School in the North was to aid the South in cutting off the abolitionists and the South was to aid in the North by cutting off the New School men.

> Without the south, the Old School Assembly of 1839 would have convened with one third fewer members. Old School Presbyterianism would have been a secession movement in 1837 and upon its leadership would have fallen the odium of schism.
>
> Having successfully held the south, however, the Old School emerged with control of a uniform, well-organized denomination capable of educating its ministry, supporting its boards, and steering a prudent course through provocations that were destined to split

[1] Smith, Elwyn A., "The Role of the South in the Presbyterian Schism of 1837–38," XXIX *Church History* (1960) 1:44–63, 57.

every major Protestant denomination except the Episcopalians before the Civil War. The price it paid was the opprobrium of being, if not a pro-slavery church, at least one which refused to take a stand on the pressing issue of the time.[2]

Like the House of Representatives and many state legislatures, many of the churches attempted to avoid the major moral issue of the day by suppressing discussion. The Presbyterian situation was more complicated than some, but the same forces operated among the Methodists, Baptists, and others.

Apart from church divisions which persist to the present day, one of the most important permanent effects of religious division was the founding of the state of West Virginia. In spite of an express Constitutional prohibition (Art. IV, Sec. 3.1), the people of the hill country of the Old Dominion formed a separate state rather than secede from the Union and were admitted as a state on June 20, 1863. The western revivals, led by abolitionists, had shaped the religious mind of the area. The people of the new state took the official motto, *Montani semper liberi* ("mountaineers are always freemen").

Popular Piety

The uncritical identification of northern piety with the Union cause was matched by the pathos of religion in the Confederate forces. Just as some of Lincoln's generals—Clinton B. Fisk, Samuel C. Armstrong, Oliver Otis Howard—were noted for their Christian faith, and later gave important leadership in the education of the freedmen, so some of the generals of the Confederacy were among the most distinguished Christian leaders American Protestantism has produced. In addition to Leonidas Pope, Episcopal bishop, John B. Gordon and T. J. ("Stonewall") Jackson were outstanding for their Christian faith and action. Unfortunately, the strength of American Protestantism was also

[2] Ibid., p. 61.

its weakness: in important segments of the churches the stress on personal decision and initiative led to definition of the Christian life solely in terms of individual piety.

During the war, camp meetings, revivals, and conversions were reported enthusiastically by chaplains on both sides of the line. Clergy and theological students were plentiful in both Union and Confederate forces. Religion and piety were appreciated, if kept individualistic. In a famous report on the gray-uniformed armies, *Christ in the Camp, or Religion in Lee's Army,* the introduction stated the perspectives:

> It was always assumed that the cause for which they contended was righteous; on it was invoked the divine blessing, and the troops were exhorted to faithful service.[3]

> The people were never more religious, and faith in God was never at a higher point. The southern people felt that their cause was just, and prayed with fervor and confidence for success.[4]

Religion was, however, narrowly defined—as though, having uncritically identified Christianity with the Union or Confederate causes, respectively, the churches were determined to avoid all other controversial issues thereafter. Conversions, when reported, involved a change from the traditional soldier's life of gambling, swearing, and drinking. The Confederate president, who was diligent in declaring various fast days and days of prayer that "the wicked designs of our enemies be set at naught," was praised by the preachers as "our Christian President, Jefferson Davis," whose proclamations "always had the right ring."[5]

On the northern side, "Chaplain" McCabe (later Bishop), went about defending the holiness of the Union cause and singing "The Battle Hymn of the Republic." Northern

[3] Jones, J. Wm., *Christ in the Camp, or Religion in Lee's Army* (Richmond: B. F. Johnson & Co., 1887), p. 14.

[4] Smith, George G., *The History of Georgia Methodism* (Atlanta: A. B. Caldwell, Publ., 1913), p. 324.

[5] Jones, J. Wm., op. cit., pp. 42–45.

Church sentiment may be captured by reference to actions of the Detroit Annual Conference of the Methodist Episcopal Church. At the 1862 meeting this body resolved:

> The annals of the past, however, stained by the blood of civilized humanity, furnish no scenes of sanguinary strife more significant of great ideas and principles, than are those transpiring within the domain of our national life. . . . On the one side are the sublime and self-sustaining forces of modern Christian civilization; on the other the decaying elements of an effete social system, combining the expiring energies of feudalism with the brutal demonstration of unmitigated barbarism. . . . The great fell disease of the south, wasting its vitality like consumption, degrading its existence like the loathsome leprosy, heating its life into burning fury like the poison of the serpent, spreading its death-producing forces like the terrible cancer, is the blood-nourished disease of human slavery.[6]

Two years later the same body denounced all wavering or compromise:

> Worse than all, we have been deeply pained at the wavering faith of some of our fellow citizens in the righteousness of our cause, and the noisy clamors of others for the speedy termination of our sufferings by a dishonorable and ignominious peace.
>
> A compromise with rebellion is treason against God.[7]

The following year the Conference rejoiced and proclaimed:

> No more slavery in these United States, and let all

---

[6] *Minutes of the Seventh Session of the Detroit Annual Conference of the Methodist Episcopal Church,* held in the City of Ann Arbor, September 24–29, 1862 (Detroit: Steam Power Printing Establishment of O. S. Gully, 1862), p. 33.

[7] *Minutes.* Ninth Session, Detroit Annual Conference. Adrian, Michigan. September 14–22, 1864 (Detroit: Steam Power Printing Establishment of O. S. Gully, 1864), pp. 10–11.

the people join to thank God for it. It is politically
dead, and constitutionally buried. . . . And that Christianity has been the great agent in the extirpation of
this evil, is a fact so clear, that it cannot fail to impress
the mind of every candid and unprejudiced thinker.
It is Christianity that has educated the National conscience up to the point of exterminating this evil, and
has said to four millions of the race: "Behold your
freedom and your God!"

They then went on to approve those actions of the federal
courts and soldiery by which southern church properties
were being taken over by the northern churches:

> *Resolved,* that we most heartily approve and sym-
> pathize with the efforts of the proper authorities of the
> Church to extend the influence of an unperverted
> Christianity, and an unsullied Methodism, in all the
> Southern states.[8]

All of this language is most revealing. The image of "Christian civilization" is securely fixed. In crisis, the Protestants
revert instinctively to use of state power to effect their ends.
At the end, the southern churches remained identified with
"the lost cause" and the churches in the North went on to
bless the national political and economic expansion which
flung the flag clear across the Pacific to lay conquest
Hawaii and the Philippines. Radical Reconstruction was
mounted on the righteousness of the northern Protestants.
A northern fireater delivered himself of the opinion that

> . . . the most unmitigated set of villains they have
> in the south are the Methodist, Baptist, Presbyterian,
> and Episcopal preachers . . . all talking secession . . .
> drinking mean liquor and advocating the cause of Jef-
> ferson Davis and the Devil.

The same feelings obtained on the other side and prevailed

---

8 *Minutes.* Tenth Session. Detroit Annual Conference. Flint,
Michigan. September 13–18, 1865 (Detroit: Advertiser and
Tribune Print., 1865), pp. 18, 20.

for years after, but on occasion at least were suitably rebuked.

> Sometime after the close of the war a southern min-
> ister spoke very bitterly in Lee's presence of certain
> actions taken by the Federal Government. General Lee
> was grieved deeply to hear him so express himself, and
> said, "Doctor, there is a good old book which . . . says
> love your enemies." Then Lee pointedly asked, "Do
> you think your remarks this evening were quite in the
> spirit of that teaching?"[9]

Unhappily, the standards of thought and action set by
Abraham Lincoln, perhaps America's greatest theological
mind in the nineteenth century, and Robert E. Lee (1807–
70), as fine a Christian gentleman as the Republic ever
produced, were far higher than the churches on either side
could understand or practice. In both sections the churches
generally had reverted to the stance of culture-religion, proclaiming the word which appeases and pleases rather than
the Word which convicts and converts.

Of the theologians of the day, Abraham Lincoln (1809–
65) (a layman and non-member) was almost the only one
who perceived the frightful ambiguity and sinfulness of the
Civil War for what it was. Where else do we find recognized the God Who is not the domesticated household god
of private persons but the God of nations and generations?
In Lincoln's writings the awfulness of the judgment of a
righteous God is understood, and nowhere else do we find
such sense of the need for forgiveness, compassion and
reconciliation between all who shared in the monstrous
wrong of fratricide and the rending of the Republic.

The Civil War represented the triumph of sectional interest in politics and culture-religion in the churches. For
a generation the southern politicians attempted to suppress the discussion in Congress, in the courts, and in the
churches. For a generation a series of nonentities held the
American presidency—Martin Van Buren, William Henry

[9] Quoted in Pitts, Charles F., *Chaplains in Gray* (Nashville:
Broadman Press, 1957), p. 120.

Harrison, John Tyler, James K. Polk, Zachary Taylor, Millard Fillmore, Franklin Pierce, James Buchanan—men whose chief accreditation was that they would not attempt to give leadership. The attempt to avoid the developing crisis by denying its existence simply created the image of the "slave power," an aristocratic cabal ". . . that control in and over the government of the United States which is exercised by a comparatively small number of persons, distinguished from the other twenty millions of free citizens, and bound together in a common interest, by being owners of slaves."[10]

Yet, even in the Deep South, only a tiny minority ever held slaves—in Georgia, only six men owning over one hundred at one time. The issue was never properly joined—in the churches or in the country as a whole—in time to prevent civil strife. The South turned to escapism. The writings of Sir Walter Scott were the chief intellectual diet of ladies and gentlemen in the ante-bellum period, and they had about as much to do with the realities of the plantation system as the interests of the poor farmers had to do with slaveholding and slave-breeding. Nevertheless, the image was created and became a political fact—both in other sections and in the South—and has persisted in some quarters to the present day.

The attempt to suppress discussion made moderation impossible and rendered the civil explosion inevitable. In addition, in the economic sphere the Deep South found itself opposing the railroads, harbors, canals, homestead policies, educational grants, and other national programs free labor was demanding for the development of the Mississippi basin. It was this force, which the cleverest southern politicians had striven to hold in check, which tipped the balance.

The broad Atlantic slope is one continuous plain.
The immense basin of the Mississippi includes, as the

[10] Quoted in Stampp, Kenneth M., ed., *The Causes of the Civil War* (Englewood Cliffs, N.J.: Prentice-Hall, Inc., 1959), p. 3.

bosom of a common mother, the states from the Lakes to the Gulf of Mexico . . . the country is thus physically one. . . .[11]

The farm boys who gave Grant his bloody victories came from the new Middle West, and they represented a developing society which for a hundred years was to hold the political balance of power in the U.S.A. (1860–1960).

The Middle West as a Puritan Power

The Middle West became the center of a transplanted New England Puritanism. The Yale "Bands" which in the middle decades went out to Illinois, Iowa, the Dakotas, to found churches and colleges and establish Christian civilization on the prairies set a certain cultural and political as well as religious pace. The Congregational preachers were so prominent in the organization and leadership of the Republican party that the Copperheads attempted to win the immigrant Irish and German Catholic support by appealing to their fear and resentment of New England Puritanism. Clement L. Vallandigham and his allies attempted to develop a politics based on western sectionalism, standing over against both northern and southern sectionalism. A number of prominent editors backed him with their newspapers, and the "peace movement" reached its zenith at the high tide of the Confederacy (1863). Rev. Billingsgate Smith, editor of the Dubuque *Union*, attacked Lincoln at every opportunity and made his name synonymous with unreasoned and intemperate politics. The Dubuque *Herald* attacked the Emancipation Proclamation as "the crowning act of Lincoln's folly."[12] The Detroit *Free Press* was a Copperhead organ, and also the *Illinois State Register* of Lincoln's home city of Springfield. So was the *State Press* of Iowa City. But the Copperhead cause, which at one time and

[11] Ibid., quotation on p. 51.
[12] See Klement, Frank L., *The Copperheads in the Middle West* (Chicago: University of Chicago Press, 1960); quotation from p. 43.

another controlled several state legislatures, was crippled by having a number of prominent leaders who were anti-immigrant and anti-Catholic and helped to drive the new settlers from Europe even more strongly to the Union cause which, as free laborers and farmers, they were inclined toward anyhow. In the East, Samuel F. B. Morse was a prominent figure. Billingsgate Smith was a violent anti-Catholic and Know-Nothing, too. Thus the struggle between abolitionists and Copperheads in the Middle West tended to shape up as a quarrel between two Protestant parties, with the revivalists again scheduled to win over the nativists and standpatters.

Sectionalism in the Churches: A Form of Culture-Religion

The failure of avowed Christian statesmen to accept responsibility for the whole people and for the universal church appeared early, and has continued late. John C. Calhoun's last speech, read in the Senate in opposition to the admission of California, is representative.

> I have now, Senators, done my duty in expressing my opinions fully, freely, and candidly, on this solemn occasion. In doing so, I have been governed by the motives which have governed me in all the stages of the agitation of the slavery question since its commencement. I have exerted myself, during the whole period, to arrest it, with the intention of saving the Union if it could be done, and if it could not, to save the section where it has pleased Providence to cast my lot, and which I sincerely believe has justice and the Constitution on its side. Having faithfully done my duty to the best of my ability, both to the Union and my section, throughout this agitation, I shall have the consolation, let what will come, that I am free from all responsibility.[13]

[13] Stampp, Kenneth M., ed., op. cit., quotation on p. 29.

In this statement two things stand out: 1) the sectional attachment which plainly ranks higher than the national; 2) the lack of a sense of involvement in the sin of the society, of anything beyond individual choice and performance.

The American military chaplaincy, today more fully integrated into the system of rank, pay, dress, and administration than either British or German military chaplaincy, is another example of the way in which the American Christians have habitually met emergency problems by reverting to close co-operation with government and unembarrassed use of taxpayers' money. It too dates from the Civil War. Until 1849, twenty chaplains had been authorized by the Army. In 1861 regimental chaplains were authorized and in 1862 Jewish rabbis were made eligible in the Union forces. During the Civil War there were eighty-six Confederate chaplains, thirty-six of whom were Methodists; like the officers they commonly supplied their own horses and equipment.

Although the chaplains devoted themselves to the needs of the forces, helped with such acute need as they could among troops who suffered far more from disease than bullets, most of the hundreds of clergymen who remained home contributed to the hatred on both sides. Their language before, during, and after the war was considerably less Christian than Abraham Lincoln's; the President's words and actions remained, with the exception of Generals Grant and Sherman in the terms of surrender they extended the southern armies in defeat, almost the only leadership profoundly conscious of the truly biblical dimensions of the tragedy. The genuinely reconciling spirit of the great representative figures of the struggle—Lincoln, the man of the new Middle West, and Lee, the gentleman of old Virginia —was rendered powerless by the failure of the white churches to preach repentance, reconciliation, forgiveness. Lincoln was murdered, his program replaced by the policy of revenge. Lee was isolated, his name to become a catchword of vulgar demagogues and cheap racialists.

After the war the church statements still revealed bewilderment. The southern conventions and conferences denied their sin and complicity, and expressed no words of repentance or forgiveness. The northern churches were equally righteous in identifying the cause of religion with their own interests; after the murder of Abraham Lincoln, a considerable section supported the policy of vengeance which he had hoped to prevent. For a fatal century the southern churches nourished the myth of the lost cause and the northern churches enthusiastically identified with national expansion and aggrandizement. In that section of Protestantism which had been most influential during the first half of the nineteenth century—the Methodists, Baptists, Christians, and Presbyterians, it was the Negro churches that kept alive the Word that convicts and saves.

The Advance of the Christian Negroes

In spite of desperate poverty, general illiteracy, severe moral problems stemming from earlier tribal life and exacerbated by slavery, the Negroes moved forward in three generations to a high level of Christian life. The Negro preachers continued to enjoy a leadership role among their people which the white ministry was rapidly losing. The Negro spirituals made known and appreciated throughout Christendom by the Fisk Jubilee Singers (f. 1876) and groups like them, have been America's only major contribution to Christian music and liturgy to the present day. At the present time some of the most distinguished Christian leaders in the U.S.A. are Negroes, and the percentage of the Negro population adhering to the faith is the equal of that in the white population. Their loyalty to Christianity while under pressure has been remarkable. Although from 1928 on the Communist Party made a determined appeal to dissatisfied Negroes, the relative percentages of CP membership have always been higher for the whites. Today, during the tensions surrounding the problems of integration in the military forces, public conveyances, schools, etc., there is ample evidence that Christianity is a more formative force in the behavior of the Negroes than it is in the white communities.

When the war was over a number of Lincoln's generals devoted their lives to the education of the freedmen. General Samuel Chapman Armstrong, founder of Hampton Institute, undertook his work as "a more patriotic, more difficult work than fighting for my country." General Clinton B. Fisk was identified with the great university which bears his name. General O. O. Howard was in charge of the Freedmen's Bureau, which dispensed some fifteen million dollars before closing—usually working through church organizations and boards for the care of the freed slaves. A great university in Washington, D.C., which by 1940 had received a total of $17,000,000 in Congressional appropriations, bears Howard's name. Here again, as in other emergency situations, such as Indian affairs, we find that American Protestants have consistently reverted to governmental action and the use of taxpayers' money when forced to deal with new situations. In spite of the popular myth to the contrary, Protestantism has not stood solidly for "separation of church and state" and voluntary support of church work. On the contrary, the movement toward a consistent pattern of religious liberty and voluntaryism has been as difficult —and as punctuated by reversions to type—in Protestant circles as among Catholics and Jews.

Reconstruction ended in tragedy for the Negroes and for the Republic. In 1876 Governor Samuel J. Tilden of New York (Democrat) won the presidency, but the election was close and depended upon the determination of disputed electoral votes. By a "gentlemen's agreement" between the Republican minority and southern white machines, and a straight party-line vote in the Electoral Commission, the Republicans took the presidency in exchange for "granting the southern Democrats the right to restore white supremacist control of the south."[14]

---

[14] Conrad, Earl, *Jim Crow America* (New York: Duell, Sloan, and Pearce, 1947), pp. 174–75; Logan, Rayford W., *The Negro in the United States* (Princeton: D. Van Nostrand Co., 1957), p. 40.

In 1877 President Rutherford B. Hayes abandoned Reconstruction and made a good-will tour through the South in the course of which it was made clear that the Fourteenth and Fifteenth Amendments to the national Constitution would not be enforced. The unseemly alliance of northern Republican reactionaries and southern Democratic machines continued as a major factor in the disfranchisement of the Negroes until the beginning of reforms under Franklin D. Roosevelt, and was again the controlling force in the Eisenhower administrations (1952–60).

In the meantime, however, the Negroes more than justified the confidence placed in them by the Republic and the churches. Although the old style Negro preacher has been alternately a subject of humorous report and patronizing comment, there can be little doubt that the faith of Negro Christians had a biblical scope and grandeur sadly lacking in the white churches of North and South in the half-century following Emancipation. The deliverance out of bondage, the year of jubilee, the mighty works of the God who frees and renews—these were the subjects of the Negro sermons and spirituals, while religion in the defeated South turned to private piety and in the expansionist North to manifest destiny.

Taken as a whole, the Civil War was the most traumatic experience in American history, and particularly in the history of religion in America. Even the Great Depression did not leave a like impress upon the soul of the nation. It was the first modern war, studied as such by German and British military tacticians. It was the first war in which a man was killed by machine-gun fire. It was the first war in which ironclads fought. In it the first ship sunk by a submarine was counted. Battles involving unparalleled masses of troops were conducted. There were 115 regiments which suffered 50 per cent casualties in a single battle. With two and a half millions in Union uniform and one million in Confederate gray, more Americans were killed in the Civil War than in all other American wars put together—from the Revolution up through the Korean conflict. One out of four in Confederate uniform died, and for two generations the wasted and ravaged Southland paid a bitter price for taking up the sword.

A Softened Evangelism

In the postwar period, mass evangelism continued to be dominant. There was, to be sure, argument about continued use of the old forms. But Sunday School conventions, Chatauqua, and a host of other new techniques were introduced and used by those who turned away from the camp meeting. As revivalism became popular, the message of repentance was softened. The harsh words of judgment which had once brought anxiety to the hearts of the sinful and aroused a desire to turn again to a new life were moderated. Nor was the preaching of the Word softened by accident: for example, recent research has documented the charge that businessmen promoted the 1857–58 "prayer meeting" revival in order to divert the people's attention from their moral duty to the slave.[15] Unfortunately, a spurious revivalism has often been used in this fashion. In the 1930s, while Harry Bennett's thugs were using violence against labor in the Ford plants the company was paying off "evangelists" in Detroit and Dearborn who condemned collective bargaining as an instrument of Satan but never mentioned the word of the Bible about the fate of those who make the measure small and the shekel great, and grind the faces of the poor. Liston Pope's classic study of a southern milltown, *Millhands and Preachers* (1942), showed how during the same period in another industry the priests of production (Baal) cloaked their shamefulness in the language of a pseudo-revivalism. But this, like Dwight L. Moody's avoidance of all reference to social is-

[15] Smith, Timothy L., "Historic Waves of Religious Interest in America," *Annals of the American Academy of Political and Social Science* (1960), No. 332, pp. 9–19, 11.

sues,[16] was a betrayal of the great tradition of revivalism and mass evangelism.

In its great period, revivalism was directed toward a verdict and a change in the personal life and a renewal of society fit for the New Men and New Women of redemption. As tragic as the betrayal of the revival tradition itself was, the discrediting among many cultured intellectuals of the whole work of evangelism has been even more serious. For the American churches have lived from evangelism: from camp meetings through to radio and TV preaching and house-to-house visitation, the methods of popular evangelism have sustained and formed American Protestantism. It was this motif which freed the churches from time to time from dependence upon the old political strategies, which made voluntaryism and missions possible.

This activity of evangelism or home missions was the only way the people could be won back to the church after the collapse of the state churches. It was the natural function of a voluntary system of membership, the method which replaced the old coercion and persecution. And the most crass type of popular evangelism is, after all, vastly preferable to the use of the sword to enforce conformity. What was needed of the intellectuals was appraisal and analysis, help to the churches in consolidating the vast gains thus made. All too often, however, the betrayal of the full Gospel by some who used the language of the old-style evangelism has turned the educated and cultured away from the catechetical work which was their manifest responsibility. They forgot that the Gospel must be communicated in the language and at the level of apperception of those to whom the Word is directed.

The new anti-clericals did not perceive that those who used the old language to serve slavery, or "private initiative," or "the American way of life," were in fact perverting the Gospel and betraying the great tradition of revivalism

[16] Ibid., p. 14. Professor Smith's fine work, *Revivalism and Social Reform* (1957) is the definitive work on the relation of the great social crusades of the nineteenth century to classical revivalism.

in America. They did not themselves understand that the word of true evangelism is not this bad word that everything must stay exactly as it is but the wonderful and emancipating word that all things are being made new. Thereby many cultured despisers of the evangelism which made voluntaryism possible in American religion have all too often left the ordinary folk and their problems in the hands of a primitive leadership, or have only dealt with the problems of Christianity and the common life in essentially secular terms.

This was the real tragedy of the Fundamentalist-Liberal split: that those who maintained the tradition of evangelism became all too often the tools of economic privilege and allowed the uncompromising Gospel to be muted and blended with folkways and mores; while those who maintained the universal claims of the God of nations and generations (as well as families and individuals) embraced all too uncritically the form of words and secular ideology prevailing in the centers of culture and sophistication.

The rapid growth of the churches was accompanied, indeed in part accomplished, by the abandonment of traditional standards of discipline. The record of the Methodist Church in this respect is representative. At the time of the American Revolution, the predominant churches were the Congregational, Anglican, and Presbyterian. By the time of the Civil War, the Methodists had grown to a position of public prominence in both North and South. Bishop Matthew Simpson of the M.E. Church was a close friend of leaders of the Republican Party, and distributed patronage in Indiana. Abraham Lincoln looked to him for advice, and he preached a bitter funeral oration at the graveside of the murdered President. Chaplain McCabe, later Bishop, was a leader in the United States Christian Commission which provided food parcels and special services to the Union troops. In the South the Methodists were equally well established. In neither North nor South were real standards of membership maintained.

On the frontier the Methodists, like the Baptists and Disciples, grew far more rapidly than the Congregationalists or Anglicans or Unitarians. The latter denominations insisted on an educated ministry, which slowed their growth. More important, the rapidly growing groups were those which were accustomed to building their membership by direct appeal and were organized to support their work on a voluntary basis. A valiant effort was made for a time to maintain standards of preparatory membership and to sustain the disciplines within the fellowship which made confessional, ethical, and moral witness possible. The Methodists remained for a time a church ruled by standards higher and better than those prevailing in the society at large. Indeed, the church courts provided the chief disciplinary agencies at various times.

Separate sittings for men and women were maintained into the 1840s in some conferences, and many Methodists wore simple clothes. The custom seems strange to most church people today, but a powerful social reform was involved. Formerly, in the established churches, the leading families owned their own pews, and the common folk sat or stood in the back. Having the men sit on one side and the women on the other meant segregation by sexes, but the end of segregation by class status. Like the Moravians, the early Methodists agreed that status in the world came to a halt at the door of the Church. But all this was changed as popularity and statistical success blinded the churches' eyes to the question of maintaining disciplined witness, opposed when necessary to the prevailing mind and mores.

Indeed, the most important negative consequence of the successful mass evangelism has been the elimination of standards of membership. It is this which has brought the major Protestant churches to their present predicament. When their membership was smaller it was more significant. Their theological and ethical and organizational discipline was also stronger, even though the problems with which they dealt in a semibarbarous society were tougher and harder to handle. The break to culture-religion was finalized in Methodism by the change of membership standards in the General Conference of 1908 (M.E. Church). The six months' probation in class was struck out, on a motion put by Daniel Dorchester:

> Omit the words, "a leader with whom they have met at least six months in class," and insert the words, "the official board or the leaders and the stewards' meeting, with the approval of the pastor."
>
> Amend by striking out the words in the latter portion of the first section reading, "under the care of proper leaders for six months on trial" and insert the words "properly recommended."[17]

Church discipline, so important to Free Churches, was abandoned in the other major denominations about the same time. One of the chief reasons for the breakoff of conservative church groups in this period, although frequently articulated in terms of confessional orthodoxy, was actually the abandonment of membership standards in the denominations which had expanded so successfully during the period (1801–1906). The larger churches thus enter the period of theological and ethical conflict, in the twentieth century, without disciplined troops and without a clear understanding of the line of battle. This is the major price paid for the enormous statistical success of a century and a half of mass conversions. The problem is like that of every mission field where a multitude of new Christians confronts the church with a flood of unbaptized beliefs and practices.

In the Methodist movement the doctrine of Christian perfection has led to many divisions. Frequently these divisions have been attributed to some other factor. But we gain a true perspective when we realize the way in which all discipline has been weakened during the century and a half of mass evangelism since the collapse of the colonial state churches. Charles Finney and "the Oberlin theology" were more Methodist than Presbyterian. The Free Methodist division (1860 ff.) was ostensibly in opposition to the autocratic episcopacy; in fact it was *pro-perfection*. In 1867 the National Association for the Promotion of Holiness was

[17] *Journal of the General Conference of the Methodist Episcopal Church* (New York: Eaton & Mains, 1908), p. 542.

formed at Vineland, New Jersey, and colleges were founded at Olivet, Asbury, and Taylor University, Indiana. Again, the issue was whether Christian perfection was an integral part of Christian doctrine and practice.

In 1894 the Bishops of the Methodist Episcopal Church warned the denomination against the emphasis, but the warning did not halt the devotion of the faithful. In the next decade no less than ten different bodies separated from the Methodist organization, persuaded that the denomination had sacrificed the original Methodist emphasis on perfectability. The bifurcation continues to the present day: in 1946 the Evangelical Methodist Church was founded. Again, the reason was not merely resentment of the power of the episcopacy: those involved were convinced they were standing up for Christian perfection. The conflict was between churches with discipline, any discipline, and promiscuity of membership.

The growth of church membership as a result of successful mass evangelism has been astonishing, comparable to few other periods of church history and surpassed by none. Always the accession of great numbers has been accomplished on a mission field, and always the "new Christians" have brought over into the church some of the habits of their unbaptized condition. This is the fundamental fact about the course of American church history, the fact which brings our churches into the category of "Younger Churches." Once a part of European Christendom, and to be discussed in that setting, the American churches are now above all products of a century and a half of successful mass evangelism and characterized by the problems to be expected of "new Christians": vague and unprecise theological orientation, morals and ethics set by cultural and tribal mores rather than according to Christian standards, frequent disloyalty to church pronouncements in case of conflict with prevailing class or national prejudices, etc.

This brings us to the nature of the crisis, and it is an utterly different situation from that of a declining European Christendom. Sometimes it is said that our churches are on their way to becoming social establishments, if not legal establishments. A better way of putting it would be through reference to the language of the mission fields rather than the language of traditional Western Christendom. Our problems are those of newness, freshness, undisciplined energy, undirected dynamic. The threats to the faith come from prophetic aberrations of the sort often found on second- and third-generation mission fields, from inspired prophets and cults which combine some Christian teachings with tribal or cultural values. Among the Indians of the Great Plains it was once the Ghost Dance religion; in Africa at the beginning of the century it was a cult movement on the Ivory Coast; among Negro Americans there have been, among others, the hyphenated messages of Marcus Garvey and Father Divine; among whites we have the deviations of Mary Baker Eddy, Norman Vincent Peale, and "Christian Economics."

Mormonism

America's three original contributions to the infinite variety of the world's religions are Mormonism, Christian Science, and Jehovah's Witnesses. As bizarre as they are according to the norms of classical Christianity, all three function freely as "churches" in American society and their members enjoy the same rights at law as citizens in more familiar traditions. Indeed, the highest ecclesiastical officer ever to serve in a key post in the national government was a member of the Council of Twelve of the Church of Latter-Day Saints (Mormon)—Ezra Taft Benson, Secretary of Agriculture under President Eisenhower.

Mormonism is best understood as one of the many variant movements which sprung from Puritanism, both in England and in America. In the fields of politics and internal economic organization its greatest leaders have shown energy and genius of the highest order. Their style has been that of many other prophets and patriarchs that sprang from radical Puritanism. To this day, in the desert areas which they have subdued, cultivated, and civilized, the Mormons display that pattern of political, economic, and religious effort which recalls the standing order of the early settlements in New England. In fact, it is not too much to say that the largest intact carry-over of the old Puritan establishment is now to be found in the Mormon settlements of Utah, Nevada, and other sections of the western Great Plains. From their rules against tea, coffee, tobacco, and liquor through to their ingenious tithing system they carry on the tradition and atmosphere of old New England. Not that the New England Puritans maintained exactly such rules; but their zeal to bring everything under subjection of the rule of Christ, their fixity of purpose and unbending zeal, later expressed itself in this way.

The claim that Joseph Smith, Joseph Smith, Jr., Brigham Young, and Ezra Taft Benson are sons of old New England may need some more detailed justification. We may take Mormonism as an example of the perpetuation of the New England way in the West after it disappeared in New England.

What was Mormonism, and how and why did it arise? The movement arose in the "burnt-over district" of the revivals in western New York. This was a district which gave rise also to the Seventh Day Adventists and other religious communities of strong "we-feeling." The weakness of the revivals came to be the "hit-and-run" style of their conduct, with insufficient attention being given to follow up in training groups, class meetings, local congregations. Many of the later revivalists were as inconsistent in their thinking as those of the Great Awakening and Second Great Awakening. On the one hand they had come to accept the practical consequences of the fact that America was a mission field, unchurched and yet to be won to Christ. On the other hand, there was the traditional self-deception implicit in American messianism—that America was a Christian nation, different in style and spirit from the old Egypt (Europe) out of which her people had come. Even the Methodists, who had been warned by John Wesley that to convert without following through with class meetings and careful instruction was but "to breed children for the murderer," grew increasingly careless in their standards of membership.

The assumption seemed to be that those won to the faith would find their normal place in existing institutions or be satisfied with new denominations operating in conventional ways. The situation called for much more drastic measures, however, and the neglect of consistent discipline on a voluntary basis led to all kinds of new movements and religious deviations.

The rapid founding of new denominations was not the result of mass evangelism itself; it was a result of the failure of older and more established churches to provide for those who had come alive beyond the point of being satisfied with religion as one of the substantive elements in American society. As on other mission fields where European Christendom failed to pursue the logic of its own message of discontinuity, so in America too the "new Christians" either fell back in a short time into the old way of life or were gathered up in new prophetic cults which blended tribal wisdom with selected or corrupted Christian teachings.

In upstate New York, in the 1830s, folk wisdom was largely derived from old New England. Joseph Smith's message offered a solution to those who had looked in vain to the revivalists for food to sustain their awakened spirits, for a new pattern of community to express their new faith.

Joseph Smith (1805–44), prophet and proclaimer of the "fullness of the everlasting gospel," was born in Vermont of a family with two centuries of Massachusetts history. He belonged to that society which, in breaking up, produced the founder of the Shakers, "Mother" Ann Lee (1736–84), and Jemima Wilkinson (1753–1819), "the Universal Friend." In the "burnt-over area" of the revivals in western New York state he received the revelations and on April 6, 1830, founded the Mormon Church. In the brief years remaining to him before he was martyred by a mob at Carthage, Illinois, he laid the foundations of one of the most remarkable communitarian societies in western religious history. He gathered his first followers in the area which also produced William Miller (1782–1849) and the Adventists, John Humphrey Noyes (1811–86) and the Oneida Perfectionists, as well as the True Wesleyans and other persons and societies combining revivalism and abolitionism.

Characteristic of the camp meetings and revivalists was their ethical earnestness. They worked through the area year after year, however, converting and reconverting, without giving clear and careful guidance to newborn men and women as to how to continue their pilgrimage in responsible churchmanship. What was lacking was an institution like the Methodist "class meeting." The recently disestablished Anglican communion was totally inadequate to serve the western part of the state and the nearly 90 per cent unchurched fell readily into the hands of those who gave them practical leadership in realizing the "new life" announced by the revivalists. Joseph Smith, anti-Catholic and anti-Masonic, stressing the Covenant with Old Testament vigor, with the characteristic Puritan attitude on care of the poor and destitute and toward material prosperity in the life of the saints, capitalized on the racial memory of ex-New Englanders and on the emotional drive of a new people strong to carve out a new life in a new nation.

According to Smith, the saints were in a literal sense descendents of Israel. The doctrine of the covenant was carried back behind its universal and prophetic enlargement to the tribal phase. A special status was defined for the American Indians. Although the Mormons were vigorously opposed to slavery, they taught that the black skins of the Negroes was due to divine displeasure and punishment. Within their tribal covenant, the Mormons have no place for the darker races of the earth. Within the people of promise there are levels of authority, and within groups of peers a radical egalitarianism. Government in their councils must be by consensus, not by parliamentarian majority rule. All who have the call are entitled to preach; the priesthood of the laity is taught and practiced. To this day, young men who satisfy the requirements go by the hundreds for two year periods of preaching, at their own expense, to the far corners of the earth. There are now Mormon churches in all of the major cities of Europe, although the heroic period of the movement was certainly the settling of Utah in the middle of the last century.

The settlement of the desert, one of the most dramatic episodes in America, came as a result of conflict between the Mormons and "Gentiles" further east. Although mob violence cannot be excused, candor requires the admission that the Mormon theocracy did not lend itself to good relations with neighbors who did not share their views and practices. Joseph Smith turned more and more to political action in the west. Nauvoo, Illinois, was practically a state within a state—with separate government and militia. Smith's hostility to slavery and loyalty to the national government were expressed in his 1843 proposal:

> The Constitution should contain a provision that every officer of the government who should refuse to extend the protection guaranteed in the Constitution should be subjected to capital punishment.[18]

In the Presidential election Smith had supporting groups in twenty-six states, opposing both Whigs and Democrats. Although his own pursuit of political power developed gradually, and matured with his conviction that persecution of the Mormons could not be stopped any other way, it simply served to enhance the suspicion of outsiders.

Even after Smith had been martyred and Deseret had been settled on the far frontier, the suspicion of the Mormons continued. *Harper's Magazine* published the widely held prejudice:

> . . . The kingdom of Utah is composed of foreigners and the children of foreigners. . . . It is an institution so absolutely un-American in all its requirements that it would die out of its own infamies within twenty years except for yearly infusion of fresh serf blood from abroad.[19]

[18] Durham, G. H., "A Political Interpretation of Mormon History," XIII *Pacific Historical Review* (1944), 2:139.

[19] Mulder, W., "The Mormon Question: An International Episode," IX *The Western Political Quarterly* (1956), 2:417.

As loyal as the Mormons were to the Union, and as helpful as Brigham Young (1801–77) and his men were in keeping the Indians under control and maintaining an open road to California, President Buchanan strove to play down the slavery issue by catering to the anti-Mormon hysteria. Mormon universalism lent itself to misinterpretation by those who did not share it.

> The city of Zion, with its sanctuary and priesthood, and the glorious fullness of the gospel will constitute a standard which will put an end to harrying creeds and wranglings by uniting the republics, states, provinces, nations, tribes, kindred, tongues, peoples and sects of North America and South America in one great and common bond of brotherhood.[20]

This view of the future, which led their enemies to accuse them of secretly dealing with the British for a northwest empire, was after all nothing but what earlier Americans from Cotton Mather to Thomas Jefferson had held.

At one fatal point, however, Joseph Smith denied universalism and reverted back behind culture-religion of known types to tribal religion of a special kind. This was not the practice of polygamy, a passing phase of Mormon culture. Essential in his teaching was the myth that the faithful were in a literal sense descendants of Israel. In following this reading, the *Book of Mormon* applied the promises only to those who came within certain special racial groups. Excluded were the Africans and Asians. American Indians and Jews were relegated to special status. While Mormon representatives have scoured the archives of Europe to determine the ancestors of the saints, which by special dispensation are included in the promises, the majority of the world's peoples are still excluded. By couching their understanding of peoplehood in tribal terms, the Mormons have permanently limited their religion to a certain society and era in the history of white civilization.

Mormonism is a characteristic expression of certain

[20] Durham, G. H., loc. cit., p. 140.

views of virtue and expectation which belonged to a fixed period of American history. Without vacuums created by frontier revivals, which did not unite the new converts to structures of discipline and community, without the New England background, Mormonism would never have appeared.

Christian Science

Christian Science is not always laid to the credit of American religious ferment, since it is based on a simplified reading of the tenets of German Idealism. Evil has no real existence. Positive, manifest prosperity is a mark of triumphant living and divine favor. Like "New Thought," "The Church of Spiritual Science," and other related cults and movements, Christian Science has reduced religion to a set of simple propositions quite detached from classical Christianity's emphasis upon a personal God, historical Revelation, Incarnate Word, known Savior, Day of Judgment, final Kingdom. The Lord's Supper, revealingly enough, is reduced from partaking of blessed elements to "spiritual communion" without any material bread and wine.

When Mary Baker Eddy (1821–1910) founded the movement she had but a handful of followers in a poor suburb of Boston. By the time of her death there were churches in all of the major cities of Europe and America, and the movement had taken on the marks of prosperity which characterize it and its followers to the present day. Her teaching of spiritual healing was a neglected emphasis in the dominant churches. Her stress on the evidence of spiritual well-being in material prosperity fitted neatly the enthusiastic sense of well-being of the American businessman. Although Christian Science releases no statistics, Charles Braden's figures are probably the most reliable available:

1906	85,717
1926	202,098
1936	268,915

It is predominantly an urban movement, with 28 per cent of the membership in cities over 50,000 and 32 per cent in cities between 10,000 and 50,000.[21]

Christian Science is an inflexible movement. No original preaching is allowed: a Board of Lectureship supplies authorized interpretations. Censorship, control, and correction are provided by the Committees on Publication. The Mother Church in Boston has complete control of all organizational matters. The most important contribution of Christian Science to the life of those outside the fellowship is *The Christian Science Monitor,* one of the most reliable newspapers in the country. Religious issues are not, however, subject to discussion and Christian Science representatives do not normally participate in interreligious discussions on campus, in councils of churches or in the round-tables of Christians and Jews. More serious, they have sometimes used boycott and other economic pressure to suppress books and articles which express judgments of Christian Science which they regard as unfriendly. Most serious of all, as librarians and archivists across the country well know, early documents of the movement—as well as later critical commentaries— have to be kept under lock and key to prevent mutilation. Even written discussion is viewed with hostility.

Jehovah's Witnesses

The Jehovah's Witnesses are a third representative type. Whereas the Mormons capitalized on the dominant churches' growing neglect of brotherhood economics and practical community, and the Christian Scientists stressed the neglected dimensions of healing, the Jehovah's Witnesses stressed the eschatological note. Beginning as the International Bible Students Association, with a peculiar view of the last things, the movement has developed into a powerful proletarian cult in both America and Europe. Little is known of its exact membership, since statistics are held secret, but on both sides of the Atlantic the Witnesses have

[21] Braden, Chas. S., *Christian Science Today* (Dallas: Southern Methodist University Press, 1958), p. 190.

been able since the war to stage massive rallies with tens of thousands of adherents pressing in upon a single city. In 1949 it was reliably estimated that they had a quarter of a million members in West Germany alone.

Most Americans are only aware of this movement when traveling evangelists come to the door to offer literature or to play records to those who will listen, when they encounter salesmen of the *Watchtower* on the street corner, or when they read with amazement of the gathering of huge assemblies of Witnesses at Atlantic City or Yankee Stadium. Rarely, perhaps, may they read with astonishment and reluctant admiration of the hundreds who have suffered—or suffer today—imprisonment, brutality, and death at the hands of Nazi or Communist totalitarians. For the Witnesses are a proletarian movement in the classical, not Marxist, sense of the word: they are in the society, but not of it. They have their own language, their own secret wisdom, their own interpretation of social forces and political events, their own special clue to the direction and ultimate meaning of history. Like the Fifth Monarchy Men of Cromwell's time or the revolutionaries of Münster, Westphalia (1534–35), they are certain that the times are approaching their climax and that the numbered ones will participate decisively in the final Armageddon of history.

The founder of the movement was Charles Taze Russell (1852–1912). Originally a Congregationalist, he founded his first group of followers in 1872. His movement, incorporated in 1881 as the Watch Tower Bible and Tract Society, claimed to represent a restitution of primitive Christianity. Included were the practice of primitive Christian communism among the disciplined faithful at the Brooklyn headquarters (Bethel House); teachings include an imminent Second Coming with Millennium to follow. They are unrestrainedly anti-Roman Catholic. The name "Jehovah's Witnesses" was introduced by "Judge" Rutherford, "Pastor" Russell's successor, in the international convention of 1931. Joseph Franklin Rutherford (1869–1941) dated the beginning of the final age with 1914, the year Christ was said to have secretly returned to earth. His booklet *Millions Now*

Living Will Never Die (1920) proclaimed the message
that the end of the evil times was at hand; the movement
has attracted substantial followings from the lower economic groups in both urban and rural areas. They do not
vote, hold office, or perform military duty—although they
intend to fight for the Kingdom against Satan when the day
comes. They are not Christian non-resistants, but rather
"Maccabean Christians" in waiting.

The "Native American Church"

In addition to the three American movements mentioned, reference may also be made to the "Native American Church of North America." With few exceptions, of
which the Moravian settlements (*Gnadenhütten*) were perhaps the most important, the record of white treatment of
the American Indians has been one of consistent injustice
and insensitivity. The Puritan experiment with the Christian
Indian villages has been discussed.[22] The tribes east of the
great river were pressed westward if they survived disease,
starvation, and attack. Occasionally Christian conscience
spoke up, as in the attempted defense of the Cherokees and
Creeks by the Quakers and the U. S. Supreme Court
(*Cherokee Nation* v. *Georgia*, 1830). Even here the landgrabbers and swindlers, aided and abetted by politicians
up to the President himself, triumphed. As later in the
South Seas, white "Christian civilization" came to the in-
digenous population in the form of whisky peddlers, gun-
runners and landgrabbers. The tribes and their leaders
succumbed wholesale to measles, tuberculosis, venereal dis-
eases, whooping cough, scarlet fever, and the common
cold. Where a more humane policy was adopted, usually
under some dedicated Christian missionary, the normal
church members all too often showed themselves unable to
understand the peculiar social and economic organization
of the Indians. White culture-religion was almost as dangerous to them as the unabashed aggression of treaty
breakers.

[22] Supra, pp. 7–12.

The Bureau of Indian Affairs presents an almost unre-
lieved record of destruction of Indian social and cultural
integrity. Genocide wouldn't work with the Plains Indians,
so they were pressed into smaller and smaller enclaves.
From 1877 the bureau reduced the power of the chiefs by
introducing direct feeding of families, taking over the judicial functions of the old men, and insisting on division of
communal lands where possible. The program was summarized in the 1889 Report of the Commissioner of Indian
Affairs:

> The tribal relations should be broken up, socialism
> destroyed, and the family and the autonomy of the
> individual substituted.[23]

The reservation boarding schools, often operated by
churches on contract for use of tax monies, trained bilingual
"hostages" who were unfitted for constructive tribal leadership and unable to find general acceptance in the dominant
white society. Although some effort was made under Franklin D. Roosevelt, in the years following 1934, to assist the
Indians to find an economic and cultural existence which
respected the unique qualities of Indian life, the last great
spoliation of the Indians was carried through as part of
the wholesale raids on public lands, water power, and forests under the Eisenhower administration.

The Native American Church—"Peyote Cult"—is the most
vigorous attempt of the Indians to meet white "Christendom" by means of a prophetic movement like those frequently encountered on missionary frontiers in Asia and
Africa. Tenskwatawa, "The Prophet," brother of the great
Shawnee chief Tecumseh (1768?–1813), was one of the
earliest leaders of such resistance. During the second half
of the nineteenth century a profusion of syncretistic reli-

[23] T. P. Morgan in *The Annual Report* of the U. S. Bureau of
Indian Affairs (Washington, D.C.: U. S. Government Printing
Office, 1889), pp. 3–91, 4. On the general record see Fey, Harold
E., and McNickle, D'Arcy, *Indians and Other Americans* (New
York: Harper & Bros., 1959); Collier, John, *Indians of the Amer-
icas* (New York: Mentor Books, 1948).

gions appeared on the Great Plains: the "Grass Dance," "Hand Game," "Ghost Dance," etc., cults. Of these the Peyote cult alone has survived in comparative strength, adopting some aspects of Christianity (Ten Commandments, Golden Rule, the Jesus figure) and attempting to shape Indian resistance to white cultural hegemony by a type of Pan-Indian nativism.[24] Like the "Christendom" which it opposes, the Native American Church is a form of culture-religion—a ghetto which cannot survive the challenge of a genuine universalism when (and if) it appears. Like the "Black Nationalism" of some Negro semi-Christian or Moslem cults, its existence is due to the recurrent reversion of American Protestantism to white tribal religion and is prima-facie evidence of the failure of the white churches to maintain the integrity and witness of the universal church. So long as the church remains "the most segregated institution in American society,"[25] it may be expected that various cultic ghettos will stand forth to be charged to its account.

In spite of the pain caused, it must be said quite candidly that the movements mentioned were all in some sense sincere—if misguided—efforts to reassert neglected elements of biblical truth. Christian Science, for example, spread rapidly because of the widespread neglect of the New Testament truth of healing by the power of faith. Today the experts in mental health are content to assure us that much illness of apparently physical nature is in fact psychosomatic in origin. But in the heyday of rational religion, miracles and mysteries were scorned in many churches. An Episcopalian leader, Dr. Elwood Worcester, started the "Emmanuel Movement" to restore the emphasis on the mission of healing. But the word fell on stony ground in the established denominations. More specifically, the reason the ". . . Emmanuel Movement did not meet with

[24] Slotkin, J. S., *The Peyote Religion* (Glencoe, Ill.: The Free Press, 1956), passim. See bibliography, pp. 143 ff.
[25] Pope, Liston, *The Kingdom Beyond Caste* (New York: Friendship Press, 1957), p. 105.

widespread acceptance by the clergy was because it required too much preparation on the part of the busy pastor of a congregation."[26] It is a sobering thought that the pattern and course of American Protestantism might have been quite different, might have never known the cult of Christian Science, had the leaders of the churches given renewed attention to the ministry of healing in time.

So too with Mormonism and Jehovah's Witnesses, as aberrational as they are in terms of classical Christianity. We cannot deny that the casual identification of American individualism with Christianity was also aberrational, and that the Mormon emphasis on the Covenant history of a select people—however bizarre in some particulars—was a neglected truth. The nineteenth-century continuum of Christ and American culture was a false religion, too. And however incredible and literal-minded the JW's peculiar doctrine of the Kingdom may seem, we should not forget that in biblical religion the advent of the Kingdom is a moment of dramatic penetration and reversal of the normal course of human expectation. The particular style of democratic progressivism to which much American culture-religion was addicted is also heretical. The Kingdom does come "like a thief in the night," not like the last benevolent administration in a long era of good feeling.

Positivism and Pietism

At the end of the nineteenth century, church membership had climbed to 35.7 per cent of the population. In the process of making such striking gains, the great revival churches had largely abandoned internal discipline, both theological and ethical, and accommodated themselves to the prevailing spirit and mores of the times. In the North and West, the appeals of a vigorous economy and culture could scarcely be withstood. Not all went over to the particular style of muscular Christianity which Theodore Roosevelt preached in *Fear God and Take Your Own Part*

[26] Scherzer, Carl G., "The Emmanuel Movement," II *Pastoral Psychology* (1951) 11:27–33.

(1916) and other tracts for the times. But even the noblest proclamation, as represented by Walter Rauschenbusch (1861–1918) and the "Social Gospel," was inherently optimistic and immanentalist.

> The social gospel has an inherent interest in history. Individualistic theology sees everywhere countless sinful individuals who must all go through the same process of repentance, faith, justification, and regeneration, and who in due time go to heaven or hell. . . . This religious point of view is above time and history. On the other hand the social gospel tries to see the progress of the Kingdom of God in the flow of history. . . .[27]

The "individualistic theology" which Rauschenbusch criticized was more at home in the South, where churches which had lost their grasp of major public issues in identifying with the defeated Confederacy were turned inward toward individual and familial religion. Here the Pietism which was earlier blended in with the Puritan thrust tended to separate out again. Unlike the northern churches, which shared in the social reform movements and progressivism of the times, the defeated southern churches came to concentrate more and more on the "true inwardness" of religion. At first, in the heyday of the Modernist-Fundamentalist disputes and heresy trials, the battle lines were often drawn between those who subordinated Christian belief to "scientific philosophy" and those who were defending a genuine—if somewhat dehydrated—version of orthodox dogma. "The Fundamentals" about which many conservative Christians rallied were propositions; and the Christian Word is not propositional but a Life. Nevertheless, the old fundamentalist line, atavistic and scholastic as it was, was closer to Christianity than the simplicistic summarizing of the faith in a discipleship without scars and a church without the cross: "What would Jesus do in a case like this?"

In the North the social concern, the other side of the Puritan tradition, expressed itself in various ways. Symbolic

[27] Rauschenbusch, Walter, A Theology of the Social Gospel (New York: Macmillan Co., 1922), 2d edition, p. 146.

is the fact that clergymen were instrumental in founding the American Economic Association, the American Sociological Society, the American Historical Association, the Modern Social and University Settlements Movement, etc. In the South religion became more and more introverted, shifting from Fundamentalism to latter-day Pietism with the steady decline of Bible reading in the homes and membership instruction in the churches. Today, although the old phrases are frequently repeated, it is clear that the objective tests and validations have been largely abandoned. Most of the magazines and spokesmen claiming to defend the great tradition of revivalism are in fact heartily affirmative toward the unbaptized society and its power structure; many of them have accepted the status of pensioners of the world, and earn their pay by attacking those who are experimenting with new methods in the evangelism of social structures.

The fact is that both positivism and Pietism were the characteristic products of the nineteenth century's abandonment of the path of disciplined witness and acceptance of a continuum of Christ and culture. They were two sides of the same coin, neither worthy of the great tradition. And in both sections, whenever grave problems arose the churches quickly reverted to the action pattern of Protestant establishment. They still thought of themselves as the dominant tradition, speaking for the Protestant people of a Protestant nation. "Protestant moralism," against which Reinhold Niebuhr has inveighed so consistently, is simply the posture of churches which speak to and for the whole population in the same tone of voice which they direct to their own memberships. The irony of the situation is that the less the churchmen were able to speak in the name of solid and well-disciplined memberships the more they spoke as leaders of a "Protestant nation."

The Triumph of Home Missions

So the nineteenth century drew to a close on the calendar without the Protestant churches realizing that the situation had changed radically: i.e., that they no longer spoke

for solid constituencies, and that the Republic now numbered large minorities of Jews and Catholics for whom they
had no mandate to speak at all. Moreover, the carry-over
of the idea of America as a Protestant nation blinded the
eyes of church leaders and public alike to the truly remarkable thing which had happened: the most successful century of missions and accession of "new Christians" anywhere at any time in church history. Because of the false
myth of the Founding Fathers as devoted Christians
and champions of religious liberty, because the American
churches still thought of themselves as part of the European Christendom whose high point had been the sixteenth
century, much preaching and exhortation took on the color
of talking about the "good old days." Looking backward,
the Protestants looked fearsomely at the newer immigrants
when they regarded them at all. The closeness of ranks
which they no longer had on a voluntary basis now could
be recovered in part only by two devices: 1) by appealing
to Protestants against the Catholics and Jews; 2) by appealing for the churches' support of some particular piece
of legislation. Both of these negative lines served to obscure
the fact that America never had been Protestant or Christian either, in anything but name, and that in spite of theological vagaries and flaccid memberships the Protestant
churches had the strengths and potentials of newness as
well as its dangers.

Over a century ago the great scholar Philip Schaff expressed in prophetic words the special potential of the
American religious setting:

> The glory of America is a free Christianity, inde-
> pendent of the secular government, and supported by
> the voluntary contributions of a free people. This is
> one of the greatest facts in modern history.[28]

Schaff, whose education and extraordinary perception as
church historian made him one of the ablest interpreters

[28] Schaff, Philip, *Germany; Its Universities, Theology, and Religion. . . .* (Philadelphia & New York: Lindsay & Blackiston/
Sheldon, Blakeman & Co., 1857), p. 105.

of European and American religious life, looked to the day when the American potential would be understood and realized. Voluntaryism was indeed the genius of the American churches, but up to this day its implications have neither been fully realized nor even accepted.

Many contemporary writers attempt to read back into the past a "wall of separation" between church and state which in fact never has existed in the United States. Indeed, the form of words, the shibboleth, is a major impediment in the way of honest discussion. Take for example a book published by Beacon Press in 1950, which attempts to document such "separation." Two of the most striking quotations are the language of the 1896–97 appropriation act for the District of Columbia and that of the Smith-Hughes Act of 1917. In the former case

> . . . it is hereby declared to be the policy of the Government of the United States to make no appropriation of money or property for the purpose of founding, maintaining, or aiding by payment for services, expenses, or otherwise, any church or religious denomination, or any institution or society which is under sectarian or ecclesiastical control. . . .[29]

In the other, a special section is cited:

> No portion of any moneys appropriated under this Act for the benefit of the States shall be applied, directly or indirectly . . . for the support of any religious or privately owned or conducted school or college.[30]

These and other selections are used to build up a climax:

> . . . so in all civil affairs there has been a complete separation of Church and State jealously guarded and unflinchingly maintained . . . this involves no dis-

[29] Butts, R. Freeman, *The American Tradition in Religion* (Boston: Beacon Press, 1950), quoted p. 145.

[30] Ibid., p. 144.

crimination between individuals or classes. It invades
the religious rights of no one. . . .[31]

The conclusion supposed to be drawn from such argument is that America, once having "had" religious liberty,
is in danger of falling away from it into various unworthy
compromises of principle. Usually the Roman Catholic
Church is blamed for attempts to remove the ancient land-
marks so wisely laid down by the Founding Fathers. Occasionally, more broad-minded authors point out that in
significant areas the Baptists and Methodists too are falling
away from the standards of the past. Even as magnificent
a study as Winthrop Hudson's *The Great Tradition of the
American Churches* (1953) makes the same assumption:
separation of church and state once existed and is now
threatened by various sorts of legal and cultural compromise. Professor Hudson's study, so worthy in principle and
purpose, is thus set in a faulty reading of the course of
American history.

The genius of American church history is rightly stressed
by Schaff and Hudson. But religious liberty and a "wall of
separation" are not identical and—in fact—we have had neither. After fifteen hundred years and more of established
Christian religion it is only natural that the break to voluntaryism should take time and that there should be culture
lags and reversions to type in attempting to develop a new
style of relating church and society, religion and politics.
What we have in fact had is a carry-over of many sorts
of establishment from the past, some unquestioned even
yet and others still being fought out. The fact that Congress
felt under compulsion to include such sections in the legislation as those cited is simply proof that the issue existed.
Federal tax monies were then being used, as they have been
used throughout the history of the Republic, for the support of religious organizations and institutions, and it is this
fact which makes the disclaimer in the 1896–97 Appropriation Act for the District of Columbia and the Smith-Hughes
Act of 1917 intelligible. The romantic myth of a "wall of

[31] Ibid., p. 176.

separation" simply confuses the issue. What is needed is less myth-building and more attention to the realities of the problems before the Republic.

These realities are given by the nature of American church life as a successful field of missions, not by some supposed falling away from an earlier state of virtue.

CHAPTER IV

American Religion at Floodtide

It might be said that the churches, agonized and shamed by their sectionalism and division, greeted World War I with relief. Here, confronting a foreign enemy, was a good cause on which they could co-operate again with a will. That they did so, enthusiastically and uncritically, is a matter of record. Ray Abram's *Preachers Present Arms* (1933) has documented the way in which thousands of preachers identified American national purpose with the Gospel of Christ. The strange ambivalence of American foreign policy, swinging between isolationism and the crusade, was dramatically illustrated in the support given Woodrow Wilson, Christian, who tried to keep us out of the war (aided by the pacifist, William Jennings Bryan) and then turned American energy "to make the world safe for democracy" (aided by Robert Lansing, a new Secretary of State, with another point of view). The myth of the New World, drawn out and away from the European "Egypt" of power politics, class discrimination, and ceaseless warring, which the churches have done so much to create, has come to afford little assistance in girding America for the long, tedious, day-to-day business of responsible leadership in a complex world scene.

European Metropolis and American Frontier

Sidney Mead has suggested that "in the shaping of the American mind and spirit, space has thus far overshadowed time in formative significance."[1] There is much in this observation, for the growth of national consciousness was accompanied by the sense of distance from the Old World and the excitement of unlimited frontiers yet to conquer. Nevertheless, the colonies and the new Republic have remained bound to the basic concepts of the Old World— in tension, and sometimes in violent reaction, but without yet having broken out of the frame of reference of Christendom.

Among American historians, none has more suggestively discussed the implications of the frontier for the style of American life than Walter Prescott Webb of the University of Texas. In *The Great Plains* (1931) and *The Great Frontier* (1952), he described the way social and political and economic history were shaped by the relationship of the frontier areas to Europe and by the "fault-line" in America which distinguishes life on the plains from that east of the Mississippi River. His findings, when applied to the religious scene, produce striking results.

During the last four and a half centuries, the relationship of Europe to the rest of the world has been that of the metropolis to outlying districts. From a static society numbering about 100,000,000 people scattered over 3,750,-000 square miles in 1500, Europe exploded in population and scattered across the globe. The Industrial Revolution, combined with exploitation of America, Asia, and Africa, coupled with a vastly improved system of food supply and medical care, launched the European peoples on the road to great increase in population and improvement of living standards. Not until about 1930 did the population catch up with the boom in new wealth and the ratio of population, land, and capital revert to the proportion of 1500. The

[1] Mead, Sidney E., "The American People: Their Space, Time, and Religion," XXXIV *The Journal of Religion* (1954) 4:244.

dynamic interaction of metropolis and frontiers, which Professor Webb believes to have reached its terminus about 1930, determined the style of life in America and other colonies of Europe during this period.[2]

This is a sound way of putting the religious posture as well. Church history in America illustrates the thesis that until recently the mind-set of Americans was determined by dependence on or reaction to the European pattern of Christendom. This was as true of the Protestant churches after disestablishment as it was of the colonial state churches. Most seminary courses are still taught in the shadow of the sixteenth-century Reformation and the policies of churches are set by formulae fixed in the Augustana (1530), in the Westminster Assembly (1643–49), etc. The same may be said of the Catholic and Jewish communities, which have functioned as ghettos within the dominant culture. With all of the vitality of the American concept of a moving frontier, the religious bodies here have remained attached psychologically to the metropolis long after the actual patronage and control ceased to exist. Only within our own time has America begun to shift from a monochromatic Protestant mentality to a conscious tri-faith pluralism. Will Herberg's brilliant study, *Protestant-Catholic-Jew* (1955), marks the beginning of the coming of age of religion in America. The self-understanding of churches and synagogues, so fundamental to a sound theology and discipline of witness, is now being worked on in the livest circles of all three major faiths. And whatever the continued indebtedness of the American religious communities to European universities and lay movements and sister churches, it is evident that the base of operation for all three major faiths has shifted. America has become the heartland, no longer the appendage to the "metropolis" of Europe.

In his earlier study of the Great Plains, Professor Webb revealed a "fault-line" in American history which is just as significant for interpreting the development of religious his-

[2] Cf. Webb, Walter Prescott, *The Great Frontier* (Boston: Houghton Mifflin Co., 1952), passim.

tory as the idea of metropolis and frontier. And, although the general theory of the influence of the frontier on American church life has been thoroughly exploited, Webb's special contribution has not. His hypothesis, so important for any understanding of American cultural history, he has summarized as follows:

> From the study emerged the recognition of a far-reaching truth, a principle of wide applicability. It was that the Great Plains environment . . . constitutes a geographic unity whose influences have been so powerful as to put a characteristic mark upon everything that survives within its borders. Particularly did it alter the American institutions and cultural complexes that came from a humid and timbered region. . . .
>
> The failure to recognize the fact that the Plains destroyed the old formula of living and demanded a new one led the settlers into disaster, the lawmakers into error, and leads all who will not see into confusion.[3]

The Great Plains

In sum, Professor Webb shows that as they emerged from the humid, timbered land of the coastal and trans-Allegheny areas into the arid stretches of the Great Plains, the settlers were forced to adopt new tools, new styles of building, new legal codes, new property concepts, new social institutions. Where they failed to do so, they ran into disaster. Among the survivors a new civilization emerged, different in kind from that of Europe—which had successfully transplanted itself into early America of the coast, the Northwest Territory, and the old South.

> European civilization has developed largely in a forested region rather than in a plains environment.[4]

The log cabin couldn't cross the Mississippi River, and

[3] Webb, Walter Prescott, *The Great Plains* (Boston: Ginn & Co., 1931), p. vi.
[4] Ibid., p. 29.

neither could cotton or slavery. In his famous March 7 speech Daniel Webster pointed to the logic of the new land where new states were emerging:

> And I now say, Sir, . . . there is not at this moment within the United States, or any territory of the United States, a single foot of land, the character of which, in regard to its being free territory or slave territory, is not fixed by some law, and some irrepealable law, beyond the power of the action of the government.[5]

Webster's words of moderation were resented by extremists on both sides, but he read the signs aright so far as the Great Plains were concerned. The artifacts of the Great Plains were the six-shooter (the ideal weapon for a horseman), the barbed-wire fence, the windmill, the land grants for railroads and colleges, dry land farming. Slavery was not part of the future of the trans-Mississippi area.

The "fault-line" in American religious history corresponds in a striking way to the "fault-line" which Professor Webb discovered and pointed out to general historians. For it is in the area of the Great Plains that religious voluntaryism and pluralism have been most readily accepted and are becoming institutionalized in various ways. When Protestantism left the area in which it was established and privileged, it had to make its way on its merits. Contrary to the situation in the Atlantic coast states, where there are still carry-overs—particularly in the state universities and public institutions—of the old connection of church and state, in the Great Plains religion is frankly voluntaryistic and pluralistic. On occasion, to be sure, religious bodies have attempted to use state power to affect their ends. Particularly has this been true of those sections where some religious group has been dominant in state or county or local life, carrying over the New England style—as on occasion with the Baptists, Mormons, Presbyterians. But the newer immigrants, even when they have been concentrated

5 Ibid., quoted on p. 190.

as are Catholics and Lutherans in certain states and counties, have been remarkably circumspect about abusing their advantage. The Southern Baptists are much more open to criticism, as were the Presbyterians earlier. How this is so can readily be established by reference to the history of the westward movement and the developing patterns of religious co-ordination in state universities. More than any other institution, perhaps, the universities reveal those images and values which a society makes its own.

The Rise of Secular Higher Education

It is significant that the great change in American higher education should date from the Morrill Land Act of 1863. This was enacted during the period of the social revolutions brought about by the Homestead Act of 1862 and the Emancipation Proclamation of January 1, 1863. In the long run, the vast cultural and educational forces set in motion by the educational bill may affect the course of religion in America more than the other two put together. For it was the massive land grants of the Morrill Act which shifted the center of gravity in American higher education from Christian and humane purposes to secular and pragmatic goals. Today, two thirds of the Ph.D.s given annually in this country are granted in the Big Ten universities. And, although most of them are given for theses on such vital subjects as coal tar, synthetic dyes, acetates, and structural stress, there is still room for more dissertations on religious subjects than presently in progress at the old centers such as Harvard, Yale, Columbia, and Princeton. The large state university does not avoid religious research and publication: it simply assumes—with the exception of Iowa's School of Religion—that it will be handled without regard to the integrity of the theological discipline.

Ironically, it was the misguided piety of revivalist Protestantism which—as in the founding of the technical colleges and universities in nineteenth-century Germany—gave the first great impetus to the state colleges and universities. The pious were determined that their sons and daughters should receive the technical training they needed in order to make their way in the world and equally determined that they should not be exposed to the hazards of classical and liberal learning. So the state colleges were voted massive subventions by the Federal Congress and state legislatures controlled by Methodists and Baptists and Disciples and others who wanted their children to have training in agricultural science, mechanical engineering and other "useful" skills without the danger of exposure to Greek philosophy, Latin letters, Roman jurisprudence, and other classical pursuits.

Theology was deliberately eliminated, both because there were few capable of handling the discipline in its catholic and universal dimension and also because the American university was at this very time undergoing a major structural change. The structural change was fundamental and affected the basic patterns of higher education. It is usually stated that what happened was the founding of the first graduate schools, with Daniel Coit Gilman at Johns Hopkins University and Andrew Dickson White at Cornell University pointing the way. What actually happened was far more fundamental, although it was related to the development of the university as a center for research. The shift from general Christian and humane purposes for all students to departmental specialization and vocational training was the main event, with the development of the graduate school but the capstone to the process. Symbolically, the old Master of Arts degree (M.A.) of the British and New England schools was superseded by the Ph.D. of the German universities. The classical view of the university as a fellowship of teachers and students (*universitas magistrorum ac scholarium*) was overpowered by the post-Humboldt view of the university as a laboratory and research center.

The reform of the American universities was led by men who had taken their graduate degrees in the great universities of the nineteenth century: Berlin, Göttingen, Tübingen, Marburg. In the process, the graduate school and professional schools reached down into the undergraduate program and dominated those years and studies as

well. Most fateful, from the point of view of religious concern, was the elimination of theology as an intellectual discipline. The Puritan and Pietist churches had already
prejudged the issue, in their eagerness to maintain the protectionist approach, by setting up many of their theological
seminaries in small villages or out on the countryside away
from the perils of the open dialogue. But it was the state
universities of the Middle West, shy of any relationship
which might seem to savor of the establishment of religion,
which completed the isolation of American theology from
the main centers of academic effort. In the Continental universities, theology was an accepted discipline and the theological faculty led the academic processions. Even though
separate, as medicine, law, philosophy, and the arts were
separate, theology could carry on its efforts within the general framework of the university and the rules of discourse
provided by the society of the learned. In America, however, the old Christian and humane tradition was liquidated
and it was replaced by a truncated academic system which
rigidly excluded theology. For several generations, now,
American university students have continued their intellectual development during the college and graduate years to
reach extraordinary levels of competence, but their intellectual grasp of theological issues has remained atrophied at
the level of adolescent emotion.

At first, the churches were happy to have it so. They were
suspicious of philosophy, hostile to those ideas emanating
from the university which did cross lines with religion;
many were opposed to an educated ministry altogether,
and saw no reason for worrying about the level of lay theology either. There were those, however, who saw how dangerous the total effect could be. Learning would become
emancipated and secular and, cut off from its roots and
ultimate responsibility, frivolous. Theology, separated from
alternative ways of thinking and being, would become im-
poverished, esoteric, and irrelevant. That such a dichotomy
actually occurred was clearly evidenced during the Funda-
mentalist-Modernist controversy.

The earliest colleges and universities were established as

chartered corporations, although during the period of the colonial state churches they received tax support. Following the model of Harvard and the other Christian foundations, the earliest state schools also emphasized Christian and humane education. The pace was set by the private foundations. When the Dartmouth College case (1819) determined that these foundations could not be taken over by the legislatures in direct control, additional impetus was given to the establishment of state schools. However, the tradition of the establishments was such that public subventions were long given universities basically Protestant in orientation. Harvard, with its Divinity School, continued to receive grants from the Massachusetts legislature until 1834. On the other hand, the state university which became Rutgers University had the New Brunswick theological seminary of the Reformed Church of America as a constituent part until 1856. Even today, Rutgers has a Protestant chapel and a Protestant chaplain—as do many of the state universities of the thirteen founding states. The University of Virginia had compulsory Protestant chapel through the Civil War and the University of South Carolina continued the same tradition through World War II. Here is but another area in which the Atlantic coast tradition of Protestant established churches carried on long after the "separation of church and state" was supposed to have occurred.

What we have in this history can be illustrated geographically. The Atlantic coast schools for long functioned, and many of them, both public and private, still function, in terms of Protestant establishment. For a time many state universities of the old Northwest and Middle West imitated the older institutions, with their tradition of Christian and humane education. Even today, when state universities in the old Northwest Territory begin to take religion seriously, there is the temptation to revert to a pattern set in the days when the U.S.A. was a Protestant nation. Western Michigan State University at Kalamazoo has but recently erected an impressive chapel (Protestant) and installed a Dean of the Chapel (a Protestant clergyman). A similar development was forestalled at Kansas State University due to the fact that the "chaplain" appointed was sensitive to the pluralistic pattern of religion in America and developed the co-ordinator's role instead. Far more common west of the Alleghenies, however, has been the studied neglect of theology as an intellectual discipline. On the West Coast the opposition to the New England style has been so pronounced that in California, Oregon, and Washington state schools have shown great reluctance even to permit the development of significant interreligious co-operation on campus.

Thus we have today state universities in the old centers of Protestant culture still maintaining a pattern of Protestant establishment in worship, to the disadvantage of Catholic and Jewish taxpayers, and on the West Coast state schools that sometimes won't even let religious groups meet on a voluntary basis in their buildings.

Pluralism on Campus

In the Mississippi Valley and especially in the Great Plains, however, a new pattern is emerging in which all responsible religious groups are treated fairly and equally. The first break-throughs have occurred in group work and counseling, and now there is evidence that the great midwestern and western state schools are beginning to take theology seriously as an academic discipline as well. As scholars like John Courtney Murray, Gustave Weigel, Will Herberg, Robert McAfee Brown, Reinhold Niebuhr, John Bennett, and others demonstrate that Catholics, Protestants, and Jews can participate fairly in the kind of dialogue appropriate to the university campus, we may expect new advances to be made at the level of instruction for credit and graduate research.

When the Protestant churches first found themselves excluded from most of the university campuses of the Mississippi Valley, sometimes after bitter struggles to maintain their old privilege and predominance, they turned to various experiments to keep religious concern active in the university communities. From the 1880s on, the "Bible Chair" or "Bible College" was a familiar device. There are still such institutions operating in more or less successful cognate relationship to many state campuses—at North Dakota, South Dakota, Missouri, Montana, to name but a few. More successful, however, have been the student foundations. From 1923 on, Methodists, Presbyterians, Disciples, Episcopalians, and others have been busy building up centers and recruiting and training student workers to offer "homes away from home" to their constituents. Jewish Hillel Foundations and Catholic Newman Clubs have also become a regular sign of leisure time religious interest on the margins of most state university campuses.

Although some state schools have offered credit for courses taught in these foundations ("the Illinois Plan"), the most significant advance to date in accrediting religion as an intellectually responsible enterprise has been the School of Religion at the State University of Iowa. Under the gifted leadership of Willard Lampe and Robert Michaelson, this program—involving the co-operative relationship of Jewish, Catholic, and Protestant teachers paid by the several religious bodies—has grown to impressive proportions at the levels of both undergraduate instruction and graduate research. The "Iowa Plan" is without doubt the most successful effort to date to make theology an accredited part of the student's liberal education. Significantly, it is built upon a frank acceptance of the pluralistic structure of American religious life.

In many schools, over 90 per cent of state schools in fact, courses in some aspect of religion are now taught. The psychology of religion, sociology of religion, philosophy of religion, history of religions, etc., are taught in various departments. In most cases, however, they remain the hobbies of men trained in other fields. Religion is thus kept from recognition as a genuine intellectual discipline, with an integrity and disciplinary pattern appropriate to any field of learning. This is not as violently unfair as the reduction of religion to the creative use of leisure time in clubs, but it is still demeaning and disadvantageous and inappropriate to a genuinely liberal center of learning. The truth is that at the present time the leading scholars of Jewish, Catholic, and Protestant faiths are much more open to discussion, much more committed to the rules of an honest dialogue, than many of the dogmatic secularists who are determined to keep an honest handling of religion off the university campus.

In the fields of group work, counseling, and co-ordination, there have been greater advances than in the academic. Iowa's School of Religion is still a unique exception to the carefully studied neglect of religion as an intellectual discipline on the state university campuses. But in the other areas more progress has been made. The pioneer efforts in co-ordinating Jewish, Catholic, and Protestant approaches to the campus have been those at Cornell University (Cornell United Religious Work—founded by Richard H. Edwards), the University of Michigan (Lane Hall, and later the Office of Religious Affairs), the University of Minnesota, and Ohio State University (the Religious Affairs Center). The patterns of work developed on these great campuses are now being adopted more and more on other campuses with like problems.

The role of the co-ordinator of religious affairs is emerging as part of the personnel services of the state university. The co-ordinator is appointed by the university administration, not to lead worship or serve as chaplain but to co-operate openly and fairly with the leaders of the various primary religious groups: rabbi, priest, Protestant clergy, and lay representatives in faculty and student body. He is not a chaplain, but rather a lay co-ordinator of the various chaplains' work. He is generally a member of the personnel division of student services, or sometimes directly under the office of the president. His mandate usually excludes leading worship for the whole university; his "pastoral" function is not that of the clergyman but that of the educator. He is not primarily responsible to religious bodies off campus but to the university. The service which he performs not only makes for better relations between the primary religious groups than is possible where one confession has an unfair position of privilege, but it inspires the confidence of believing Jews, Catholics, and Protestants that essential distinctions are not being avoided. The dialogue on campus, as elsewhere, is based on the frank facing of differences as well as the cultivation of mutualities. Such an acceptance of the pluralistic status of religion in American society builds good faith between the primary religious groups.

Since it has been harder for Protestants, who long enjoyed a status of special privilege on many state university campuses, to accept the new style of interreligious cooperation, it should be pointed out that this makes for a much better style of Protestant effort, too. The worst enemy of positive Protestant effort has not been Catholicism or militant secularism: it has been the willingness of many who profess the Protestant position to rest their case on the preservation of reserved privileges. Protestantism on campus, as elsewhere in the Republic, is today faced with the choice between following the line of protectionism and nativism or achieving a new break-through by accepting open encounter with the various alternatives to the evangelical faith.

The most significant event in religion in higher education along these lines in recent years has been the founding of the Association for the Co-ordination of University Religious Affairs (ACURA). This professional association grew out of a decade and more of correspondence and consultation between the major centers of interreligious co-operation on campus. The initiative was taken by the director of Lane Hall at the University of Michigan and the director of Cornell United Religious Work, with the Commission on Religious Organizations of the National Conference of Christians and Jews assisting and facilitating. The first concrete result was the publication of the campus manual, *And Crown Thy Good* (New York, 1949). Then followed the three Institutes on Religion in State Universities held at the University of Minnesota, and the significant religious centennial celebrations at the University of Michigan. This last led to the publication of the volume, *Religion and the State*

University,[6] one of the most useful books in the whole field.

By 1958, a decade after the first discussions called by the NCCJ, the leading representatives of the pluralistic approach to campus religious work issued a call to all state universities similarly situated. ACURA was founded in 1959 and now has affiliates among state universities, and some public institutions with private boards, all over the country. Cultivation of the "dialogue on campus," with leading Protestant, Catholic, and Jewish scholars participating, has developed rapidly and promises a new level of educational as well as civic effort.

Experiments in Religion in Higher Education

At the level of day-to-day program, rather than at the level of structures of interreligious co-operation, the most significant break-through is occurring in experimental centers like the Austin (Texas) Faith-and-Life Community, Kirkridge, the Communities of Lay Scholars at Duke and Berkeley. Parallel to the campus programs are lay institutes like Parishfield (Michigan) and Five Oaks Christian Centre (Paris, Ontario), which are also dedicated to the difficult task of arming and equipping the laity (the whole people of God) with the discipline of intellect and witness appropriate to those who bear the name. With the appalling devotion of the major Protestant bodies to mere statistical success—and that no longer in the "fullness of time," and no longer undergirded by a real message of repentance and change of life, these experimental communities have the atmosphere and problems of "faith missions." And they carry, almost alone, the hope that the American Protestantism of the future will be more literate, more disciplined, more fully and truly the Church.

In North America and the other areas of Younger Churches the Christians are beginning to accept the responsibilities of developing a new style of Christian witness—based on voluntary support and voluntary discipline. The

[6] Edited by Erich A. Walter and published by the University of Michigan Press, 1958.

gathering of a church, self-disciplined and self-supported, is a new style of Christian life and has come into its own during the last four centuries of economic boom and expansion in which Europe was the metropolis and areas weaker politically and militarily were exploited to sustain its burgeoning population. While liberty was being born on the frontier, the established religion of the European countries was fighting desperately to maintain the monopoly which it had enjoyed during the more static Middle Ages.[7]

The American experiment was launched as a conscious break from the ways of the Old World, and it was inevitable that sooner or later a break should be made from the adjustment of church and state in which the former was an instrument of class control. The break came in some areas shortly after independence but has taken a good deal longer in others. A sound historical perspective would indicate that the American churches will come further in dealing with the unique problems which confront them if they carefully avoid the cultivation of a false and non-historical romanticism about the past. There is in many areas more genuine voluntaryism in the relation of the churches to the body politic than ever before in American history.

It is in the area of the Great Plains that a frank acceptance of religious voluntaryism and pluralism has advanced farthest. There are distinct culture lags in the area east of the Alleghenies, with state universities and other public institutions often practicing an open favoritism toward the older Protestant churches. There is certainly no sound theoretical reason why a state whose state university has an established Protestant chapel should object to providing bus service at public expense for pupils attending parochial schools! It is true, of course, that the history of religion in higher education has been different from that of the rela-

---

[7] It is significant that the most vigorous movements on the Continent, those who have mastered the significance of the rise of twentieth-century totalitarianism, should now be trying to develop the qualities of voluntaryism and lay initiative. This is the measure of the Kirchentag and Evangelical Academies.

tion of the churches to elementary (compulsory) education. But as the educational level moves steadily upward
this distinction has less and less validity.

Across the Alleghenies to the Mississippi, the old pattern
has often held on. For that matter, up until the high population mobility of World War II and subsequent years,
there were pockets of old New England in Iowa, the Dakotas, Kansas; and the happy assumptions of Methodist,
Baptist and Disciples' predominance still assert themselves
in various ways in Texas, Arkansas, Oklahoma. But the picture is changing rapidly, as the "oasis civilization" of the
arid and semiarid region begins to pass from the bare struggle for survival to an authentic culture of its own. The people to whom space is the major natural force, who cannot
survive and prosper without co-operation, turn readily to a
separation of the political and the religious covenants. Except where the oases are religiously monochromatic, the
furthering of civic co-operation between citizens of different faiths is taken for granted.

The move from the forests and highlands to the plains
was "the end of Book One of our history." The problems
faced across the Mississippi were different, although it took
long decades for the laws, religious and educational and
cultural institutions to adjust to the fact. Now there is
emerging in our national society a clear break, like a geo-
logical fault, which distinguishes the institutional life of the
Great Plains from that east of the Mississippi. The religious
life is now beginning to reflect the difference, too. In this
area, religious affiliation rarely determined political fortunes. Affiliation or non-affiliation is an open choice, and
the religious bodies depend upon voluntary support of their
members for their programs and expansion. Only occasionally, as in some sections during the 1928 and 1960 elections,
is there a relapse into the old ways of identifying religions
and political lines. But this is an anachronism in the area
of the Great Plains.

The economic development is also different in the Great
Plains, even though an earlier generation sought to stay
the tides. The attachment of Texas and the Southwest to

the Confederacy was a romantic one, though the political consequences have long lingered. Since World War II there has been growing evidence that economically and politically the Southwest is pointing toward the community of the Great Plains and away from the Southeast.

In religious life, as in other respects, the people of the plains long looked to New England or the Southeast and tried to carry over the religious style to which their fathers had been accustomed. But the tide is turning, and nowhere is it more evident than in the fact that the burgeoning state universities of the plains states are abandoning the establishment of Protestantism on campus for vigorous programs of interreligious co-ordination and co-operation.

The Decline of Standards of Membership

During the "Great Century" of Christian missions in America, two conflicting tendencies were at work in the Protestant churches. To a marked degree they still shape Protestant reactions in the new situation. On the one hand was the tremendous growth in voluntary membership, a growth which has made the Protestant churches in America the morning star of the Younger Churches. On the other hand was the tendency to hang on to the old institutions and patterns of "Christian" (i.e., Protestant) America. Thus the very evangelists who won the people back to membership often helped to perpetuate the romantic myth of the "good old days" of the Founding Fathers when America had been a "Christian" nation. Actually, it was a heathen nation at the beginning of the Republic, and a much more realistic appraisal of the achievement of the churches and their present potential can be made by admitting the fact. However, the Protestant churches have helped to cultivate the romantic myth and sometimes they are misled into fatally false action by their own image of themselves in American history. This false image, leading to false action, has affected history within the Protestant fold as well as the relation of Protestants to their fellow citizens of other faiths.

In Protestant history, the rapid growth of membership

was accompanied by a proportionate decline of membership standards. In the second half of the nineteenth century a number of church splits occurred, ostensibly for theological reasons; on closer inspection it would appear that the issue of membership standards was fundamental, with theological integrity but one of the components. With the accession of large numbers of inadequately trained "new Christians," theological and ethical and moral disciplines declined; church discipline, an essential element in any voluntary system of membership, was slackened and finally all but abandoned. Many made the natural mistake of assuming that their civic freedom, which relieved them of any obligation to support a particular church or observe a particular religious discipline, carried over into the church. Some earnest Christians, however, recognized the scandal of indiscipline for what it was. In many cases they finally separated out and formed new churches rather than be associated with, and share complicity in, a promiscuity of membership practices which disgraced the church and her Lord. Such was the origin, for example, of many of the smaller churches which split off from the larger Methodist bodies—the True Wesleyans, Free Methodists, Church of God, Holiness Association, Assemblies of God.

Unhappily, the merit of criticism of lack of discipline in the great, successful churches was often complicated by two factors: 1) an unwillingness on the part of the orthodox to accept the need for restating the fundamentals of Christian faith in language intelligible to modern men; 2) the effort of the defenders of the faith to use government to enforce certain types of orthodoxy. There is no excuse for sacrificing classical Christian convictions in order to accommodate to the spirit of the times. But there is also no excuse for hanging on to a certain form of words, as though Christians were saved by *assensus* rather than *fides*, if there are better ways of stating those truths. For orthodoxy to become dead orthodoxy is tragic indeed, for then it not only loses its winsomeness but ceases to be orthodoxy as well. The effort to use political controls when internal consensus has ceased is another fatal mistake, and it was an error into which

Fundamentalist churches readily fell in their effort to preserve and maintain essential Christian truths.

Protestant Use of State Power:
Anti-Evolution Laws and Prohibition

Nothing more reveals the temptation of American Protestants to revert to use of state power to enforce their teachings than the record of church action during the struggle surrounding the Eighteenth Amendment and the anti-evolution laws. These two issues, which cost the public careers of great and good men, and diverted Christian energy from more important matters, were fatal mistakes in Protestant action. They were wrongly conceived and wrongly executed, and above all they rested on a false presupposition: that America was still a Protestant nation and the Protestant churches had a right to force Protestant morality and belief upon the body politic. Both of them represented bad faith in public life, for they were not in fact backed by the disciplined witness of believing people. A church or other free association which has made a discipline binding upon its membership (e.g., plain dress, abstinence, conscientious objection to military service, etc.) has a right to come before fellow citizens with its witness and the recommendation that there be made a general discipline (by law) of what they have experienced and found good. Whether such legislation is then wise, if there is strong objection among other ranks of the citizenry, is another question and it must be fought out in the public forum. But in the case of both Prohibition and the anti-evolution laws this requirement was not fulfilled: politicians in the churches attempted to secure by public legislation what they were unable to persuade many of their own members was either wise or desirable. In both cases, lacking the authenticity of a genuinely disciplined witness, the Protestant reversion to political action was ultimately discredited, and the churches have not to this day recovered their authority in public life.

Let us turn first to the discredited effort of Protestant Fundamentalists to legislate certain doctrines upon the schools. Anti-evolution laws were a peculiarly southern manifestation and marked the anti-intellectual debauch of the post-World War I period much as the McCarthy hysteria and the attack on the universities symbolized the letdown following World War II. In both periods Protestant nativism played a leading role. Although the Knights of Columbus were caught up in the general attack on the "eggheads" in the retrogression of the 1950s, and the Ku Klux Klan was stronger in the period of Harding and Coolidge, the seizure was harder and lasted longer in both cases in the centers of culture-religion in the Deep South.

William Jennings Bryan (1860–1925), populist leader, was the symbol and popular leader of the fight to fasten by law a certain doctrine of the origins of man upon the schools. But Tom Watson, who built up the anti-Jewish mob spirit that led to the lynching of Leo Frank, was one of a host of lesser demagogues who rode resolutely with the debauched spirit of the times. And, lest blame be transferred too readily to the "Bible Belt," let it be remembered that it was with the approval of a president of Harvard University that Sacco and Vanzetti were murdered—by decent people who were so anxious, and who had so little faith in the American way of life, that they believed justice to two simple offbeat immigrants would mean letting the Communists take over in Massachusetts.

It was a poor time in the country's spirit and nothing showed it more than the bringing to trial of a school teacher, John T. Scopes, on July 10, 1925, in Dayton, Tennessee, for teaching evolution. The legislature, along with parallel bodies in Oklahoma, Florida, North Carolina, Texas, Arkansas, Mississippi, and Louisiana, had passed a law making the teaching of the Genesis record as a factual account of the creation mandatory, and forbidding the teaching of the evolutionary hypothesis. Bryan starred for the prosecution, and Clarence Darrow, Dudley F. Malone, and Arthur Garfield Hayes defended. The teacher was found guilty, fined, and the fine was remanded. The Fundamentalists won the case but lost the country.

At the height of the battle, Governor Cameron Morrison

of North Carolina rejected textbooks recommended by the state Board of Education with the words,

> I don't want my daughter or anybody's daughter to have to study a book that prints pictures of a monkey and a man on the same page.[8]

And Governor Miriam Ferguson of Texas, who had made herself head of the State Textbook Commission, snipped references and excluded textbooks which did not in her opinion measure up to the doctrinal standards of a certain type of primitive Protestantism. A few men, like President Harry Chase of the University of North Carolina and President William Poteat of Wake Forest, stood up to the stampede; most knuckled under. The newspapers were also weak in the face of the crisis.

Actually, the basic Fundamentalist points were far sounder than the misguided efforts to legislate orthodoxy:

1. the infallibility and inerrancy of the Scriptures;
2. the Virgin Birth;
3. the vicarious doctrine of the atonement;
4. the bodily Resurrection of Christ;
5. the Second Coming.

Although Christianity is not propositional, and intellectual assent to a form of dehydrated orthodoxy is not the soundest proof of live faith, these propositions are indeed worthy of attention and reverent discussion. They come closer to Christian doctrine than many of the opinions of modern gnostic cults. But the unhappy bent toward state churchism, and the legislation of dogmatic error to combat an hypothesis also in error if presented dogmatically, diverted attention from the real issue: the fundamental necessity that the church voluntarily maintain standards of theological discipline. The church is not, as many libertarians have erroneously assumed, a cave of all the winds of doctrine. But neither is it, in America, the religious arm of a society which can properly legislate to stop thinking with the year

[8] Cited in Furniss, Norman F., *The Fundamentalist Controversy, 1918–1931* (New Haven: Yale University Press, 1954), p. 85.

1859 (the year Darwin's *The Origin of Species by Means of Natural Selection* was published).

A Free Church is clear on the distinction between internal discipline and political enactment, between the standards to be expected of members and the prevailing mores of a society. But Free Churches are a comparatively new thing, and the tendency to slip back into the assumptions of Christendom is ever present. Nowhere is the Protestant reversion to type more evident than in the history of the Temperance Societies in America. Here, too, the revivalist churches threw back to use of local, state, and finally national government action to enforce Pietist morality. Significantly, the shift to emphasis on legislation came as the churches through statistical success could no longer count on loyal self-discipline among members.

The transition can be traced in Methodism, the characteristic Pietist and revivalist movement of nineteenth century America. John Wesley condemned "spiritous" liquors, not including wine, beer, and ale. He preached in a social situation where whisky was a major evil. In America, the Methodists held to his rule from 1784 to 1832, even though whisky was the currency of the frontier—often used to pay the preachers' meager salaries. At the famous "Christmas Conference" in Baltimore, where the Methodist Episcopal Church was founded (1784), it was recommended that the preachers take a mild ale or other aid after preaching. In 1790 the Conference removed the rule on "buying" and "selling" to meet the realities of the frontier currency situation. Through the revivals, however, the Temperance cause became securely fastened to the image of Christian behavior. Great preachers like James B. Finley and Wilbur Fisk denounced whisky and advocated the union of the Temperance Societies and the M.E. Church. Nathan Bangs and others replaced "spiritous" with "intoxicating," and total abstinence now became a rule of membership.

As the membership rolls expanded so rapidly during the nineteenth century, and instruments of brotherly discipline like the class meeting were scuttled, the internal voluntary rule became difficult of enforcement. Brotherly admonition and exhortation was replaced by legalism. The revivalists turned more and more to state legislation to enforce their convictions, and finally the Anti-Saloon League became the strongest single pressure bloc in the national political scene. By 1906, eighteen states had adopted state-wide prohibition. After a temporary recession in which local option laws were experimented with, the Anti-Saloon League, the Prohibition Party, and the Women's Christian Temperance Union combined to bring more than half of the states into the Prohibition column by 1918. By this time Congressional action had already forbade the sale of liquor in the District of Columbia and on Indian reservations, and now during the national crusade legislation was passed forbidding sales to soldiers and sailors. By the end of the year the prohibition forces succeeded in presenting legislation in the form of a national amendment to the Constitution (the Eighteenth), and it secured the necessary two thirds majority of Senate and House and was ratified by three fourths of the states.

Sumptuary legislation depends for its enforcement, however—even when enshrined in the Constitution—on public opinion. Not only was enforcement skillfully and systematically sabotaged by forces hostile to Prohibition; many of those members of the very churches which had put the campaign across in legislative form refused to be bound by it, and officers sworn to enforce it—like Andrew Mellon, Secretary of the Treasury under Harding, Coolidge, and Hoover—openly defied it. In 1933, national Prohibition was terminated by the Twenty-First Amendment.

Prohibition was the last national effort of the revivalist churches to legislate Protestant morality. Many of its great proclaimers had been leaders of mass evangelism. A number, like Gerrit Smith (Congressman; a founder of the Prohibition Party), General Neal Dow, and General Clinton B. Fisk, had also been prominent abolitionists. Not since that time have the representative Protestant churches exercised so much direct influence on legislative bodies. In a few states of strongly Protestant bent, the Prohibition cause remains—like the flurry of anti-evolution laws in the 1920s—

as a reminder of the era when the New England tradition shaped the mores of the republic. Two factors brought that period to an end: 1) the emergence of powerful communities, chiefly Catholic and Jewish, with other cultural traditions and approaches to social issues; 2) the decline of voluntary discipline and standards of membership in the Protestant churches. The period which marked the enormous statistical success of the revival churches was also the period which saw membership standards decline almost to the vanishing point. Today the Baptists and Methodists and Christian Churches don't even have enough authority to keep their members out of mob violence, let alone to hold them to difficult standards of theological or ethical or moral excellence.

Protestant Culture-Religion

Nor has the great tradition of mass evangelism carried through with unchanged ethics. It was perhaps inevitable that, as "converts" remained unchanged in life, eventually even the verbal phase should be softened and accommodated to popular opinions. Even in those circles where the old language is still current today, the great tradition is no longer operative. The perversion of evangelism can be illustrated in the career of the Rev. Sam P. Jones of Georgia. Early revivalism had not hesitated to deal with major issues in society, had proclaimed the Lordship of Jesus Christ over all of life, had called upon men to repent, convert, and be healed. In the latter half of the nineteenth century, various professional evangelists introduced a new style of message; avoiding any offense to the ruling elements in the cities, their patrons, they concentrated on the "sins" of the workingmen: drinking, swearing, gambling, and joining unions. Nor was classical conversion stressed any more.

> Jones considered the mere fact of enlistment in his army tantamount to conversion. Conversion, as he defined it, was not so much a change in belief or the acquisition of grace through faith as a change in moral

conduct, a resolution, as he put it, to 'quit your meanness' and to fight for decency in your community.[9]

Thus Sam P. Jones set the pace for the many "evangelists" to come who have eviscerated true evangelism, evangelism which convicts and converts and provides the foundation for a New Life in person and in society. Those who were fighting the first efforts of workingmen to establish collective bargaining and job security found such "evangelists" useful tools. Jones was brought to preach a "revival" at the time of the bloody McCormick Harvester strike of 1886, was used in 1899 to assist the Republican campaign against the social-minded mayor of Toledo, Ohio, and on other occasions also calmly identified the "Gospel" with the maintenance of the *status quo* in society.

The deterioration of the Free Churches into culture-religion can be measured in various ways; one of the most striking is in the decline in great preaching. Great preaching is the proclamation of the Word that convicts and converts, that moves to repentance and to turning again to the Lord of nations and generations. Popular preaching today is sluggish, its popularity based on words which are familiar and images that had content in the agrarian society but are irrelevant to the complex societies of industrial civilization. Sometimes the vulgar control of pulpits, to prevent the prophetic message, is frankly stated. In a recent issue of the Emory University *Alumnus*, a leading citizen of Georgia has stated the proposition with unusual frankness, in writing of the clergy, that

> if their advocacy from their pulpits (in which they are, in the last analysis, the paid guest speakers) becomes sufficiently obnoxious to their listeners to cause a substantial decline in attendance and gross receipts . . . the clergyman mustn't be too surprised when the

[9] McLoughlin, William G., "Jones vs. Jones," XII *American Heritage* (1961), 3:56 ff, 84.

church fathers arrange for his transfer to more favorable climes.[10]

More often, however, the pressures are so subtly disintegrating that neither clergy nor laity realize that they are sinking back into the practices of tribal religion. The false image which American Protestantism has of itself, by and large, has led to a situation in which accommodation to popular views and prejudices has muted biblical preaching. One observer from abroad called "the silence of the American pulpits" the most impressive thing about the situation. The religious book clubs and popular books on preaching, from which the rank and file derive their amusement and scalp their illustrations, provide a substitute as effective as heroin or opium to coming to grips with real issues affecting salvation.

The struggle for the liberty of preaching has always been a struggle against patronage. John Wesley introduced the itinerancy to guarantee that the Gospel would be preached whether people wanted to hear it or not. Twentieth-century American Methodism has sacrificed the itinerancy to the jurisdictional system, whose specific purpose is to guarantee in so far as possible that only preachers will be heard who say the comfortable words. Moreover, the larger churches have now fought their way through to a point where they operate on congregational principles (wrongly conceived and without historic congregationalist checks), picking the men who tickle their ears while the smaller churches carry the full weight of the machine. In the Baptist churches, whose genius was once the accent on voluntaryism and personal commitment—symbolized and emphasized by adult baptism—the relationship of covenant and discipline has been softened to simple association; among Southern Baptists child evangelism has led to the usual baptism of children years before they have reached the classical "age of accountability." Among the Disciples and Christians the classical thrust was toward restitution

[10] Wesley, Thomas J., Jr., "Must We Integrate to Educate? —No," XXXV *The Emory Alumnus* (1959), 7:14 f.

or restoration of New Testament ordinances and discipline. Among the conservative wing the dynamics of this concern has settled back into a thoroughly scholastic type of orthodoxy. In the liberal wing of the movement, opposition to fixed credal formulae has led to a wholehearted affirmation of those ideas and views which predominate in those social strata where they have their holdings. In the Episcopal Church, confirmation—originally introduced as a substitute for believers' baptism—is now commonly granted to children of eight, nine and ten years. In the recent World War, from 52 to 80 per cent of the young men of the "Peace Churches" accepted service in the armed forces. The list of adaptations could be continued almost indefinitely; they add up to accommodation to social pressures, to betrayal of the most fundamental tenets of the churches. We are not discussing at this point the validity of the tenets, but simply pointing out that in a secular society the churches are among the most secularized institutions. Neither pulpit words nor the witness of the people has retained the Scriptural saltiness.

CHAPTER V

Mid-Century Encounter

Voluntary discipline, basic to the integrity of Free Churches, had well-nigh disappeared by the end of the Great Century of missions in North America. Those small religious bodies which had split off in defense of internal discipline were largely outside the main stream of Christian events and had little part in the efforts of councils of churches and co-operative missionary societies. Nevertheless, there were by the middle of the twentieth century evidences that the churches were headed for severe shocks in their happy affirmation of the spirit of the times, and that this might in time produce a new emphasis upon disciplined witness.

Emotionally and intellectually, large sections of American Protestantism have remained lodged in the nineteenth century. As in the Victorian Era in England and the Wilhelminian Age in Germany, a continuum of Christ and culture, of cultural mores and religious values, was cultivated and defended. Even the view of missions, so formative in the experience of the American churches, was frequently expressed in cultural terms.

In an age when world peace, world citizenship, world fellowship are the goals after which popular imagination reaches out, the only objective big enough to define the comprehensive aims of the Christian world mission is the creation of a Christian world civilization.[1]

By the middle of the twentieth century, the insecurities expressed by the Hocking Report (*Re-Thinking Missions,* 1932) had eroded much of the confidence of an earlier age in the works of Christ across the world. This was noticeably true of the larger denominations, where the missionary effort had flagged steadily over a forty year period—although the less money and personnel in the field, the grander the language became.

In this period, the smaller and more intense and more disciplined churches have come to the fore in missionary effort. From the time of the 1938 *Statistical and Interpretative Survey of World Missions* published by the International Missionary Council (ed. Joseph I. Parker), it has been evident that the main portion of finance and personnel going into the expansion of Christianity in new fields was coming from the Free Churches of America. More recent reports on Central and South America, Africa and sections of Asia, have stressed the presence of missionaries from smaller fundamentalistic and pentecostal groups— quite out of proportion to the numbers of members in the home churches.[2] After a review of the situation in Latin America and the West Indies, Dr. Henry P. Van Dusen of Union Theological Seminary has referred to these groups as a "third type" alongside Roman Catholic and classical Protestant churches. Thus the expanding edge of Christianity is not only staked out by Free Churches rather than state churches, but—to a remarkable degree—by small restitutionist groups which count the gift of the Spirit and/or the process of sanctification conclusive evidences of the existence of the True Church. They attempt to recapitulate the mission and style of the Early Church, with literal obe-

[1] Anderson, William K., ed., *Christian World Mission* (Nashville: Commission on Ministerial Training, the Methodist Church, 1946), p. 177.

[2] See articles on various countries in Littell, Franklin H., and Walz, Hans Hermann, eds., *Weltkirchenlexikon* (Stuttgart: Kreuz-Verlag, 1960).

dience to the Great Commission one of the prime points. Most of all, the churches of this "third type" have a standard of discipline, in other areas as well as in missionary effort, long since abandoned as repressive and restrictive by the larger Protestant bodies.

John R. Mott and the Flowering of Foreign Missions

There was a time, before the larger churches largely lost their discipline and sense of mission, before the division movements before the First World War, when world-view and missionary passion were still held in a tight span. Perhaps no one represented so fully the peculiar genius of Christian missions in the American Protestant tradition as John R. Mott, Methodist layman. Combining personal piety and business acumen, evangelical faith, and administrative genius, he splendidly represented in his long life that high tide of religious and cultural energy which marked the nineteenth century at its best.

John R. Mott (1865–1955), called by Kenneth Scott Latourette the greatest Christian missionary since St. Paul, represented the flowering of the American churches' missionary concern, lay initiative, and universal perspectives. And in spite of the morbid fascination which many Europeans find in the wide variety of American religions and religious associations, Mott was a good deal more representative of the genius of American Christianity than were Aimie Semple McPherson or Father Divine. Mott was a layman, converted during J. K. Studd's visit in America (March 1886), with an independent income which made it possible for him to devote his life to furthering the Christian cause around the world. In the course of over sixty years of tireless travel he visited eighty-three countries, was decorated by nineteen governments, received the Distinguished Service Medal and the Nobel Peace Prize. To bring missions to a higher level of effectiveness, he was the advocate of interdenominational co-operation. He was a key figure in the World's Y.M.C.A. (Honorary President, for life), in the Student Volunteer Movement, a founder of the

World's Student Christian Federation, chairman of the International Missionary Council (1921–42), leader in the preparatory work and founding of the World Council of Churches (Honorary President), and officer in numerous other denominational, interdenominational and ecumenical organizations and movements.

In Mott, simple piety and social concern, personal evangelism and organizational genius, were combined to a degree rare in the history of the church. His expression of the layman's vision was characteristic of the Christianity of the great American churches of his generation:

> The layman must rise up and make Christianity what it was in the early days when every Christian was a missionary in the sense of spreading the faith.[3]

Mott believed sincerely that the restoration of the practical unity of Christians was complementary to Christian world-mindedness, and that both ecumenicity and missions were basic dimensions of apostolic Christianity. In him we see the flowering of the Great Century, before world-mindedness and social concern were secularized and missions became excessively individualistic.

During the tremendous upsurge of religiosity at the high tide of the popular triumph of religion in America, when all membership standards were sacrificed for the sake of the last possible statistical successes, there occurred a proliferation of cult and sect movements. Nevertheless, the significance of this phenomenon can be exaggerated. The twelve largest churches in the U.S.A. account for more than three fourths of all Christians, and most of these bodies are affiliated with the National Council of Churches. Since 1908, the year in which the Religious Education Association, the Federal Council of Churches, and the first of the denominational social-action agencies were all established, the unitive factor in Protestantism has come to the fore. Indeed, the reunion of the churches was a fundamental part

[3] Mott, John R., *Addresses and Papers of* . . . . (New York: Association Press, 1947), VI, 349.

of the vision of the pioneers of the Social Gospel—Walter Rauschenbusch, Leighton Williams, Nathaniel Schmidt, and others—who so fully represented the nineteenth-century theology and social apologetic which triumphed throughout the period 1865–1914. The present degree of co-operation between Protestant and Orthodox church bodies has not been equaled elsewhere in Christendom, although—to a considerable extent through Mott's influence—there has been a parallel growth in the other major mission fields. Effective agencies of Christian co-operation are particularly widespread among the American and other Younger Churches.

As classical mass evangelism disappeared or turned to more subdued methods, many of the groups which continued to use the language without standing for the context of the message of repentance and conversion have become impassioned champions of the American way of life or the southern way of life. In the present controversies the heirs of the liberal tradition of culture-religion have frequently carried the message of prophetic discontinuity, while avowed "Fundamentalists" justify the *status quo*. This debasement of the great tradition of evangelism is particularly noticeable as the churches face the most important ethical crisis of mid-twentieth century: racialism in the churches and in society. Discrimination against American Negroes in the churches and in society at large are two different issues, and require different solutions, although both are products of cultural norms rather than Christian faith or democratic tradition.

A Crisis in Christian Discipline: Racial Discrimination

The effort to hold the Negro, or other minority peoples, at the level of second-class citizenship is a matter of law and constitutional liberties. Although some sentimentalists have discussed the problem solely in terms of "education," it really has to do with social structures and legal rights and must be dealt with as such. Here, the proper role of the churches is that of supporting law and order, condemning anarchy and mob action, inculcating obedience to the duly constituted authorities. Life under law, even when imperfect, is still better than life in the jungle.

Within the American churches, racialism is carried over from the unbaptized society and measures the degree to which they have accommodated themselves to the prevailing culture. As the wife of a state Supreme Court justice in Arkansas put it,

> My husband has been a Methodist all his life, but if it comes to choosing between being a Methodist and an American, he'll be an American every time.[4]

But this was not the issue, quite. In this case the choice was between being a good Methodist *and* a good American, and being a tribal religionist. But the theological problem of churches without discipline comes into stark outline in the quotation. Inadequately trained for membership, admitted without preparatory training, without the proper instruments of voluntary discipline, many members never have had the discontinuity between life in Christ and life in the world brought home to them. Here the ordinary members are less at fault than the leadership of the churches, who—though sworn to uphold the form of sound words and doctrine—neglect catechetical instruction and concentrate solely on the acquisition of more new members at any price.

Significantly, it has been the churches which were most successful in the great period of popular expansion which have had the greatest difficulty in coming to grips with the issue. The Roman Catholic Church generally has taken a forthright position, and in those situations where some members have clung to tribal rather than Christian norms —as in St. Louis and New Orleans for a time—they have been confronted by the weight of a universal church. Although traditionally American Negroes have been Protestant—and four out of five of them Baptist, there has recently developed a steady though still small shift among university graduates and Negro intellectuals to the Catholic fold.

[4] Sessions, Robert Paul, "Are Southern Ministers Failing the South?", 234 *The Saturday Evening Post* (1961), 19:82.

There are many places in the southern states where a Catholic college campus provides the only place of refuge, the only sanctuary of freedom, where Negro and white citizens can meet to discuss their common problems.

The Episcopal Church and the Presbyterian Church, with traditional programs of training and discipline, also have managed to withstand unbaptized social pressures to a considerable degree. The great revival churches, however —Baptist, Methodist, and Churches of Christ—have had grave difficulty. They have had the most rapid expansion over a century and a half, have the largest percentage of "new Christians," and have had to rely more largely upon democratic processes to achieve voluntary discipline. In some areas their traditional structures of authority and discipline have functioned. Every Southern Baptist theological seminary, for example, is integrated. In other areas, however, among congregations inclined to the heresy that the voice of the people is the voice of God, there are grievous difficulties. Most striking, perhaps, is the failure of the Methodist episcopacy—once a powerful military office for the achievement of good—to meet the challenge of the hour.

Just as after the Civil War the Negro churches preached a full Gospel while the white churches identified themselves with prevailing cultural patterns, so in mid-century the leadership most inspiring to the Christian people is coming to a considerable degree from Negro ministers and lay people. Take "the student movement," for example. For a decade and a half after World War II, the student workers and chaplains in American colleges and universities were in despair. Unlike the student revolt of the 1920s and the student social action of the 1930s, student bodies in the decade 1945–55 were docile, complacent, and uninspired. Students of this period seemed interested in little but training, jobs, and marriage. They accepted uncritically what their professors taught, and the professors themselves were intimidated and subdued by McCarthyism and other vulgar attacks on the colleges and churches. With the rise of "the student movement," however, many white students as well as Negroes have been caught up in a cause greater than self-interest, and many thousands have demonstrated and sometimes gone to jail in protest against local statutes or practices which denied constitutional liberties to groups of citizens on account of race.

In the face of cowardly bombings of homes, local abuses of police power, corruption in courts, broken oaths by officials sworn to uphold law and order, and other manifestations of anarchy, Martin Luther King, Jr., and his fellow ministers have inspired their own people to disciplined action and won many whites to their side. Significantly enough, the opposition which did not resort to open violence has cloaked itself in a false view of the Gospel. Thus during the Montgomery bus strike, the first significant non-violent direct action, those who defended the *status quo* accused Dr. King of "bringing trouble where we've always had peace," as though the Head of the Church brought peace rather than a sword. And a white preacher, E. Stanley Frazier, sought popularity by outspoken championship of segregation.

> The job of the minister, he averred, is to lead the souls of men to God, not to bring about confusion by getting tangled up in transitory social problems.[5]

Fortunately, the Negro ministers have had far more influence with their people than have the white preachers, and they have managed to keep violence at a minimum in the face of severe provocation. As a result, the white community has been severely burdened in conscience where it has not sympathized with the Negro campaign outright. And among the best of the white young people and students the movement has inspired co-operation and support of the efforts of their Negro fellow students.

A Crisis in Evangelism: The Rise of the City

The second major crisis for Protestant churches has come about through the shift from rural to industrial society, a

[5] King, Martin Luther, Jr., *Stride Toward Freedom* (New York: Harper & Brothers, 1958), pp. 116–17.

shift which at first left a major proportion of Protestant churches stranded on the deserted land. During the Great Depression, hundreds of such preaching posts and chapels were abandoned; subsequently many have been reopened by Jehovah's Witnesses, the Pentecostals, and other groups that still serve "the people of the dirt." In making the shift to suburbia, however, popular Protestantism has not abandoned appeal to the village mind and style. In the flight from the rural proletariat and the depressed inner city, Protestantism generally has remained securely anti-labor, racialist, isolationist, and nativist. Although some conspicuous individual leaders of social causes have come from the Protestant churches—particularly from conscious minorities such as the Quakers and Unitarians, Catholic and Jewish Americans have contributed far more in recent years to social and cultural progress than have the major Protestant bodies.

The image about which the churches' concept of their work takes form seems to be the re-creation of the pre-Revolutionary village as the standard form of community life. This is the ecclesiastical parallel to the romantic political dream of the "good old days," before the rise of the corrupt cities supposedly spoiled the countryside and perverted simple, neighborly politics. The happy countryside of white, Protestant, virtuous America is the misbegotten dream used to justify every corrupt nativist scheme for oppressing and exploiting those who don't fit, for maintaining the monstrous misrepresentation and malapportionment by which declining rural populations keep the majority of their fellow citizens at a disadvantage. The effort to transfer the image to the green lawns of suburbia continues, but it shatters on the high mobility and political irresponsibility characteristic of the new areas.

Against the vision of suburbia as the carrier of the grassroots faith, the tough-minded observer sees only a continuing spread of the influence of the central city, and the net of the metropolis is cast in larger and larger circles, promising ultimately to engulf us all.[6]

All of this goes on, however, with little statesmanship or even exertion of influence by the churches. The Protestant churches, and more recently the Catholics and Jews, are simply abandoning the inner city to Pentecostal and Adventist sects and following the more choice consumers into the suburbs.

In the suburbs, however, all matters of power and decision are carefully soundproofed. The basic decisions governing health, education, transportation, employment, birth and marriage and death are all made elsewhere. The suburb is a parasitical growth, and the religion which serves it tries artificially to recollect the vision of a simple rural and village life which no longer exists. In the men's club at the church a great point is made of using first names; but the men who play this game do not know the last names of those who live on the same street or just around the corner. In this greenhouse of "spirituality," with its hot pursuit of unreal emotions and sensations, there are two things which religion must not do if it would be successful: 1) deal prophetically with real persons, events, forces; 2) deal bindingly with matters involving Christian witness. The suburban church is long on verbalized "values" and short on involvement. Above all, it is "tolerant" and "free." It is the happy hunting ground of the John Birch Societies, Protestants and Other Americans United, and all the other sour humors of a frustrated and increasingly irrelevant nativism; for the "freedom" which starts in rejection of the yoke of Christ ends up in enslaved service to blind prejudice.

One fourth of the U.S. population resides today in the twelve largest population areas. One half is in 220 counties, with the rest in 2800 rural counties. In this situation a few desperate efforts have been made to reclaim the wasteland of the Inner City. Most of the church missions and settle-

[6] Wood, Robert C., *Suburbia: Its People and Their Politics* (Boston: Houghton Mifflin Co., 1959), p. 95.

ments, on which a good deal of money is spent, evolved in the period before society itself had organized staffs and programs of reclamation. They are now anachronistic both in theory and practice; but nothing is harder to kill than a good work which has outlived its usefulness. The prevailing style of Protestant work in the Inner City is, to use James Hastings Nichols' description, "sensationally inadequate."[7] At East Harlem Protestant Parish and Cleveland Inner City Parish and related experiments, young ministers and laymen bound by the vows of a group ministry are attempting to demonstrate that the faith is relevant to the heart of the metropolis. But, working with great devotion, they receive little help from the largest denominational agencies.

Late Bloomers: Lutherans and Mennonites

Perhaps the most remarkable energy to enter the Protestant scene in recent years has issued from communities previously isolated from the main stream of American society and religion. As indicated earlier, Anglicans and Congregationalists dominated the church picture during the colonial period. In the age of extraordinary expansion during the nineteenth century, the pace was set by Methodists, Baptists, Disciples, and other bodies of the radical Reformation and mass evangelism. The Presbyterian contribution, a major one in certain areas (notably in political life and in higher education), was a costly one for Presbyterian order and doctrine. The problems raised for Calvinism by the methods of mass evangelism, especially in regard to the place of children in the covenant and the role of an educated ministry, produced repeated divisions in the Presbyterian movement. The Episcopal Church, after a slow start in the first generation following independence, slowly consolidated its strength and staked out claims to pre-eminence in private secondary education, in the eastern uni-

[7] Nichols, James Hastings, "Merger for Metropolitan Mission," LXXVIII *The Christian Century* (1961), 20:617–19.

versities, in the Foreign Service, and in other leading governmental and financial circles. Its roots were not deep enough in the American people as a whole for it to be affected materially by the Civil War, and it survived the greatest crisis in American history as the only major undivided Protestant church.

With the passing of the foreign-language enclaves, and with the passing of the dominance of the great revival churches, some of the ablest and most energetic Protestant leadership is coming from church communities of Continental origin which had at first lived as ghettos in the Middle West. This flowering of a group once withdrawn behind defensive barriers was evident a generation ago in the Evangelical and Reformed Church, which gave to American Christianity such distinguished personalities as the Niebuhr brothers and sister and Paul Lehmann. In recent years the alternate processes of "fossilization" and "flowering" are illustrated by the Lutherans and the Mennonites. With the main sections of their movements isolated for generations from the main Protestant effort and influence in the U.S.A., both have begun to produce first rate theologians, scientific magazines, scholarly treatises, and significant initiative in interchurch affairs.

Lutheranism appeared early on the American church scene, chiefly in the form of Pietist communities seeking freedom for their particular religious practices in Pennsylvania. But the great immigrations came in the nineteenth century, when a surging flood of Germans, Danes, Swedes, Norwegians, and Finns brought with them the religious customs and patterns of the Old World and set them down in little colonies all over the Middle West. Eastern Lutheranism had reached maturity just before the great immigrations began, and in the person of Samuel Schmucker (1799–1873) gave considerable impulse to early ecumenical interest in the U.S.A. But the new settlers were suspicious of such tendencies and determined to maintain their languages, rituals and habits unchanged.

Great concentrations of those who fled the consequences of the 1817 Prussian Church Union grew up around St.

Louis. Naming their seminary and numerous colleges "Concordia," after the great statements of Lutheran orthodoxy of 1577 and 1580, they maintained German-language services, classes, literature, hymnology, and parochial schools. With the third and fourth generations (and two world wars in which America fought Germany), they began to emerge, use English, and confront fellow Americans of other churches and faiths. The Lutheran Church of the Missouri Synod is one of the largest churches in the U.S.A. today and has produced several of the most active and esteemed church historians and theologians in the present interchurch and interfaith discussions.

Other Lutheran churches also have carried on foreign language services for a time and within the last few years made the transition to English and participation in the American society and religious life. The largest Lutheran seminary in the country, apart from Concordia in St. Louis, is the Evangelical Lutheran seminary in St. Paul, Minnesota—of Norwegian background. In recent years the United Lutheran Council has been formed, sponsoring a vigorous and well-staffed campus ministry; co-operating with agencies such as the Lutheran World Federation and Lutheran World Service on a global scale now affords a common platform for many different synods of national origin and for their participation in wider ecumenical concerns. These agencies have come to play a major role in ecumenical discussions and activities and have performed magnificently in Europe since the war. With a rich theological and liturgical heritage, these churches recently have produced a number of outstanding men for the mid-century dialogue and have also attracted the attention of many from churches of English background discontented with the dissipation of their own traditions. There has been a pronounced leakage of young clergy from the churches which expanded most through the revivals and have most abandoned standards of membership, to the Lutherans, Episcopalians, Presbyterians.

The Mennonites, too, have come to show an astonishing vigor on the American church scene. Their history in this land goes back to the end of the seventeenth century, when religious refugees from Europe responded to the assistance offered by Penn's Frankfurt Land Company. Among them were persecuted congregations of the Swiss Brethren and South German Brethren, two wings of the Anabaptist movement which sprang up in the early sixteenth century and which had survived as part of the Mennonite movement in spite of the cruel persecution of the state churches. (American Mennonites are descended from Swiss and German families, not from the Dutch wing of the movement which gave the name "Mennonite" to the general movement. "Pennsylvania Dutch" are *deutsch*, German, not Hollanders.) The first Mennonites settled at Germantown, near Philadelphia, in 1683. In 1693 they subscribed to the first protest against chattel slavery—a tract written by the Quaker, George Keith, and sent around to various congregations as an appeal to conscience.

During the early eighteenth century the "Old Mennonites" arrived, settling chiefly in Pennsylvania and migrating slowly with succeeding generations into Ohio, Ontario (Canada), Indiana, and Virginia. Their best known centers are at Scottdale, Pennsylvania (Herald Press), Harrisonburg, Virginia (Eastern Mennonite College), and Goshen, Indiana (Goshen College and Biblical Seminary). With their plain clothes, able farming, and conscientious objection to soldiering, they early became a well-known—though removed—sector of American Protestantism. In the 1870s, the second great immigration of Mennonites arrived, now organized chiefly in the General Conference and centering in Kansas. They migrated as a result of the abrogation of their exemption from military service in the czars' armies. These were the descendents of German Anabaptists who had been, because of their genius in farming and work with the hands, invited out of the violent persecution and religious wars of Central Europe by the Russian empress, Catherine the Great. The "Russian Mennonites," some of whom came out after World War I and World War II (especially to Canada), have been less restrained in their attitude toward society at large and its cultural and technological achievements. Their chief centers are at Bluffton, Ohio (Bluffton College), North Newton, Kansas (Bethel College), Elkhart, Indiana (Mennonite Biblical Seminary).

The Old Mennonites (for two hundred years) and the Russian Mennonites (for seventy-five years) were removed from the main stream of American religious life. The term "fossil" is perhaps invidious, but the religious discipline and language barrier combined to prevent a genuine encounter with other churches and with the controlling forces in public life. In the last generation, however, they have played an increasingly important role in American Protestantism. The founding of *The Mennonite Quarterly Review* (f. 1927), one of the strongest scholarly magazines in the American theological scene, may be said to mark the beginning of the new development—important to the Mennonites themselves in self-discovery and to other Christians in raising basic questions of Christian witness. Dean Harold S. Bender of Goshen and his associates have turned a considerable number of younger men to seminary education followed by doctoral work in the best theological and historical faculties of Europe and America. Goshen itself has a significant Mennonite Research Foundation, a Mennonite Historical Library rich in Anabaptistica, a fine series of historical monographs.

The General Conference Mennonites are having a similar renaissance, heralded by the founding of the magazine, *Mennonite Life* (editor: Professor Cornelius Krahn of Bethel College), and the establishment of the annual Menno Simons Lectures. The latter have been addressed, since their founding, by Roland H. Bainton (Congregationalist), Wilhelm Pauck (Congregationalist), Franklin H. Littell (Methodist), George H. Williams (Congregationalist), Gordon Kaufmann (Mennonite), D. Elton Trueblood (Quaker).

In a major joint undertaking, leaders of the major Mennonite bodies (including the Mennonite Brethren in Christ) have recently published the four-volume *Mennonite Encyclopedia*. This is one of the most significant general reference works published under denominational auspices in

America in many decades. The Mennonite Central Committee, founded in 1920 and bringing together the united work of Christian service of some 200,000 Mennonites of the U.S.A. and Canada, has grown to be one of the stronger relief organizations in the world. After World War II it was one of the three most significant staffs and programs working in Europe. Both the *Encyclopedia* and the M.C.C. are far more substantial contributions than those made to scholarship or in relief by several denominations numbering many millions of members.

Both Lutherans and Mennonites were for long separated from the strong thrust of American church life by language differences and other more or less deliberate cultural defenses. In addition, both preferred to organize their own education for the youth. For the Mennonites, small numbers and long decades of withdrawal from the problems of government and public life added to the distance from other American churches and faiths. In addition, both movements are concentrated geographically—indicating their aloofness from the expansion and national movement of the revivalist churches. The Mennonite locations have been given. The Lutherans are concentrated in the Dakotas, Nebraska, Iowa, and Missouri. Fifty per cent or more of the church membership in every county in Wisconsin and Minnesota is either Catholic or Lutheran. But now both Lutherans and Mennonites—and similar developments could be related for some other formerly isolated communities of faith—have entered the main stream of American religious thought and service in a more disciplined and church-centered way than several of the larger Protestant bodies of English background have shown in a half century or more.

Defensive Protestantism

At the end of the Great Century of membership expansion and dispersion the churches of English background, which prevailed in the colonial period and predominated during the nineteenth century (Methodists, Congregationalists, Presbyterians, Northern Baptists, and Episcopalians), were spread throughout the country without conspicuous concentration anywhere. New England was no longer predominantly Congregational; Virginia was no longer prevailingly Anglican. Only the Southern Baptists, due to their enormous growth, actually attained a significant plurality in Kentucky, Tennessee, Texas, Arkansas, Missouri, Virginia, and overwhelming preponderance in the Carolinas, Alabama, and Georgia. The self-identification of these churches with the American way of life, or at least with certain economic strata of it, produced in the end a certain style of culture-religion not unlike that of the established churches of Europe. This is the reason for the frequent remark that these churches are "established socially if not legally" in certain sections. The analogy to Europe is misleading, however: the real point is that they still carry over the memory of the Puritan theocracy, and are inclined to act like it where they have control of public education, state legislatures, etc.

Neither the individualism and subjectivism of the main Southern Baptist line nor the cultured enlightenment of northern suburban Methodism, for example, offers any real challenge to the spirit of the times. It is intensely symbolic that two of the most vocal champions of Protestant Americanism in the 1960 election should have been a Southern Baptist segregationist in Dallas and a northern Methodist pacifist in suburban Chicago. Both united on the romantic image of the good old days of Protestant hegemony in America. They failed to grasp the most elementary fact about the American scene: that it was now pluralistic in pattern. More than that, they failed to understand that the Protestantism of America is today far better attended, supported, and participated in than were the Protestant churches at the opening of the nineteenth century. Their vision was obscured by the memory of an America still officially Protestant rather than lifted by their responsibility to the millions to whom faith and its practice were voluntary, by conviction rather than coercion.

Indeed, it has been in neuralgic reaction to the growth in significance of Jewish and Catholic communities that old-line Protestants, including the large number who have long since lost any sense of theological or ethical or moral uniqueness, have been able to retain some twisted identity. "Protestants" who have never expressed any clear, disciplined, voluntary witness to the evangelical faith, who have never perceived any dichotomy between the Christian life and the norms of a heathen society, can still suddenly remember that they are children of the Reformation when "the Jewish threat" or "the Catholic threat" (the anti-Semitism of the educated) puts in an appearance.

In this situation, having abandoned evangelical preaching and discipline, American Protestantism is rarely able truly to discover itself. Its beginning mood is "tolerance," by which is meant not the decent treatment of human beings with different opinions—which is only civilized, but the lack of clarity on basic doctrines—which is only common. These churches remember that they are "Protestant" not for some gallant and glorious new proclamation of God's promises yet to be fulfilled, but when they remember that they are *not* Roman Catholic or Jewish. Then for a passing season these "Protestants" remember that in the good old days America was officially Protestant. And in the comfortable armchairs of the Native American Club they summon up the sacred names of those who braved sea, storm, pestilence, and starvation to unite "Protestants" and other Americans against the peril of later immigrations. For a brief season the captive lion recovers the echo of his former wild roar, the spavined old racer wanders from the pasture to charge once more with distended nostrils around the abandoned race track, the hero of the great 1928 game against Siwash goes down to the field at midnight to drop-kick again from the 45-yard line! In a gallant assault on the whirling arms of Alexander VI and Torquemada our Don Quixote and Sancho demonstrate that the knights and the tourney are not yet quite dead. And here they are, in 1960, picking themselves up from the dust and wending their bruised and desolate way homeward at eve. "If only Billy had spoken up, we could have elected Dick. . . ."

The Protestant churches of the New England and Puritan tradition have carried their fight with the Spanish Armada, from season to season, into the old Northwest and the South, as part of the same baggage that has produced the pressure for Blue Laws and use of the King James version of the Bible in "their" public schools. And, looking back, they carry the racial memory of the loss of the theocracy. Today, Catholics count 50 per cent or more of all church members in almost every county in Massachusetts, Connecticut, Rhode Island, New Hampshire, and Vermont; and American isolationism in the Middle West and South is as hostile to the East as it is to Europe. Few Protestants of the "heartland of America" are aware of the degree to which their antipathy to New York and Washington, with its pronounced economic and political overtones, is actually an expression of their disgruntlement at the loss of ancient privileges.

In the Protestant underworld, anti-Catholicism is as sedulously cultivated as anti-Semitism in certain other situations. And here it combines in a curious fashion with the prejudice of the intellectuals against any religious claim presented in a binding fashion. Anti-Catholicism is, in fact, an ancient tradition in American Protestantism. Most of the colonies had laws against immigration by Roman Catholics. Only the Baptists and the Quakers then ignored Locke's theory that Catholicism was dangerous to civil government, and the latter kept them out and levied special taxes to prevent the importation of Irish indentured servants. In old New England a popular game about the fireplace was called, "Break the Pope's Neck." Reaction against the Quebec Act (1774), which sanctioned taxation to support priests and extended the boundaries of Canada to take in the Northwest Territory, was important in arousing feeling against England as the Revolutionary period opened.

Catholic Growth and Nativist Reaction

Catholics supported the Revolution more wholeheartedly than any other church group, hoping that political liberty would lead to religious liberty. Many of the new state constitutions, as well as the federal Constitution, justified that hope. But the fight for acceptance was just beginning as the Catholics reached the number of about 90,000 in 1815 (the year of Archbishop John Carroll's death). The Alien and Sedition Acts (1798) had been an expression of Native Americanism, and with the rising tide of Catholic immigration the resentment became stronger. Trouble arose first in New England and in the middle states, where contract laborers were being imported in quantity to work in the new factories. Samuel F. B. Morse and his brothers founded a newspaper to fight Catholicism. The American Bible Society joined the fray to defend use of the King James Bible in the public schools. In 1832 the New York Protestant Association was founded. Lyman Beecher preached a series of anti-Catholic sermons. In 1835, the Native American party was formed, and in 1837 the Native American Association.

By 1850, one seventh of the population of the country was foreign-born. As figures earlier discussed have shown, only 15.5 per cent of the population then had church membership, and there is no evidence that the new immigrants were any less interested than the native born. But the image of Protestant America was threatened, and from 1852 on the Know-Nothing party ("Supreme Order of the Star-Spangled Banner") grew rapidly. The Native American groups favored twenty-one years of residence before the vote might be granted and would exclude Catholics from public office permanently. In 1855 there were thirty-five states with a Know-Nothing party, and they claimed the vote of one half the population; several states were controlled by the nativists. Only the rise of the slavery controversy turned interest elsewhere and averted major civil strife on religious grounds. Even then, in outbursts of mob violence, the Ursuline Convent in Boston was fired (1834), Irish homes and two parochial schools and a seminary were burned in Buffalo (1840), and violence latent or overt threatened the new immigrants wherever they settled in the Protestant states. Just as later the free Negroes were subjected to terrorism to keep their wages low and their organizations weak, and a degenerate type of Protestantism allied itself with this effort, so the poor immigrant contract laborers were subjected to a combination of religious assault and economic exploitation.

During this period, many Catholic leaders tried to keep the immigrants in intact communities, maintaining their own languages and cultural patterns, served by priests of their own national groups, separated from the dominant groups. When the pressure in the industrial East became acute, hundreds of Catholic families were transplanted to the West by Catholic societies, to settle in intact communities in Wisconsin, Iowa, Missouri, and other farm areas of the Middle West. It was the statesmanship of men like Archbishop John Hughes (1797–1864) and James Cardinal Gibbons (1834–1921) which won Catholics their rights in the industrial East. Hughes opposed the Catholic Colonization Societies, led in the establishment of a parochial school system as alternative to the Protestant-dominated public schools, strengthened the English-language leadership and self-help societies of the working people. Gibbons championed the labor unions, defeated the drive for foreign-language priesthoods, and exercised considerable influence in Washington during a very long and distinguished career (nearly sixty years as bishop).

Only the religious progress of the Negro freedmen can compare, in the history of American Christianity, with the tremendous accomplishments of American Catholics in building churches, cathedrals, universities, and a comprehensive parochial school system, during the little more than a century of progress from immigration to full citizenship. The figures on Catholic preference run as follows:

1776	c. 20,000
1815	90,000
1860	3,000,000
1920	20,000,000
1960	40,000,000

The election of a President of Roman Catholic membership can be taken to indicate the coming of age of the faith in

America. And as Professor Martin Marty wrote in *The Christian Century*,[8] this brought the moment to Protestantism to choose between evangelical faith and the anxiety of culture-religion.

In quarters where the continuum of Protestant culture-religion held on, the lights were not too bright. Although statistically the country had long been pluralistic, religiously it was still possible to conjure up Protestant nativist reaction in many sections. On November 3, 1960, under a dateline from Lubbock, Texas, the head of the Southern Baptist Convention (9,000,000 members) let fly with a representative mixture of religious and cultural prejudice. In the midst of what was in effect a campaign speech for Nixon, he not only let loose the usual anti-Catholic blast but turned his anger on Harry Truman—a well-known Southern Baptist who had been active in trying to neutralize the unrestrained activity of Baptist preachers for the Republican candidate. In the process the denominational president—Dr. Ramsey Pollard of Memphis, Tennessee—took a public stance on church discipline even more flatly contrary to Baptist principles than his effort to dictate to fellow Baptists how to vote in the election.

> Truman was a Baptist, but I never voted for him.
> . . . Mr. Truman ought to be turned out of the church because of his language. He needs to repent of his sins. His profanity was a discredit to his nation, the presidency and his church.[9]

What a long decline from the Baptist principle of discipline based on Matt. 18:15–18!

The failure of the Protestant churches to understand and accept the implications of the "post-Protestant era" in American history can be measured in two ways: 1) by reference to the way in which Protestants are naively caught up in reactionary nativist politics; 2) by noting the ineffec-

[8] Marty, Martin E., "Protestantism Enters Third Phase," LXXVIII *The Christian Century* (1961), 3:72–75.
[9] *The Dallas Morning News* (11/3/60), Sec. I, p. 6.

tiveness of the Protestant churches on issues where they try to take a positive stand.

A reactionary nativism was evident in various campaigns to "keep America Christian" during the 1950s. The fact that America has never been a "Christian nation," except nominally during the time of the colonial state churches, was ignored and the romantic mythology of the Founding Fathers was played up. With the 1952 election the public display of simple, heartfelt "spirituality" became part of the American way of life. Skillful use of this imagery became part of the professional anti-Communist crusade, a crusade largely verbal and obviously directed at others than the Communists. A book by a prominent Presbyterian clergyman, *America's Spiritual Recovery*, was published in 1954 to herald the new age of public piety. The book was dedicated to the "leader of America's spiritual recovery," Dwight D. Eisenhower, and carried an introduction by another eminent layman, J. Edgar Hoover. In this introduction, parents are advised to send their children to the churches, for the Communists do not like the Church. Thus the "fourth religion," against which Will Herberg has warned so pointedly, a religion without creeds and without discipline, was well on its way to produce an American version of the late discredited *deutsches Christentum* of the Third Reich.

By 1960 this style of "spirituality" was playing a major role in the election. In a Board of Public Instruction election in Florida a bipartisan committee was organized by leading Protestants from every denomination to elect a "solid citizen," "successful businessman," "conservative" and "devoted American" to defeat "ultra-liberal elements" and preserve Bible reading in the public schools. The widely distributed handbill had the American flag and the Holy Bible on its cover, and was aimed at "atheists and agnostics" who were supposedly threatening "Christian America." The opposing candidate was identified with "the ultra-liberal American Civil Liberties Union," cited by the American Legion at its 1959 National Convention on these lines: "its chief activities are to defend Communists and

Communist causes and to organize opposition to the House Committee on Un-American Activities and the FBI." Moreover the opposing candidate's relatives were condemned for being identified with the "radical American Jewish Congress." Worst of all, according to the native Americans, the man opposing the ideal of Christian America was "an ACTIVE LEADER OF CORE . . . the militant Congress of Racial Equality . . . currently staging 'sit-ins' and using other pressure tactics, mostly with persons imported from the north." The "Christian" candidate pledged himself to see to it that children be taught the "priceless heritages of FREEDOM, FAITH, HONOR, LOVE OF COUNTRY, DEMOCRACY and FREE ENTERPRISE." Also, he stated his belief "that social customs and deep-rooted feelings of southerners must not be flagrantly ignored, and that extremists from out of state must be prevented from stirring up violence and antagonisms with high-pressure methods." Thus armed with a package deal, his supporters set out to rally Protestants against due process of law for "radicals," against protection of Jewish children from compulsory Protestant religious offices, against civic rights for Negroes (northerners?), and against all those from out of state not bringing tourist or retirement dollars or federal contracts.

In Texas, at the same time, the discredited "evangelist" Billy James Hargis was leading extremely well-financed "Save America Rallies," aimed primarily at the government in Washington, the National Council of Churches, and the United Nations. Billed as "Founder-director of America's largest Anti-Communist movement, Christian Crusade HEADQUARTERS in TULSA, OKLA.," Mr. Hargis was announced as "THE man in person whose writings on communism became the material in the now famous AIR FORCE MANUAL, which resulted in congressional investigation into the activities of the NATIONAL COUNCIL OF CHURCHES!" The fact is, of course, that the thoroughly discredited material led to Congressional investigation—but of Mr. Hargis himself. Those who make fortunes by breaking the Ninth Commandment of the Decalogue, however, can hardly be expected to avoid the Big Lie in other areas.

Anti-labor interests lined up loyally with the new front to defend Christian America. Full-page advertisements in the strongly Protestant areas campaigned against Walter Reuther, termed the "Moscow-trained president of the United Auto Workers (AFL-CIO)" and against the Catholic candidate for the presidency who was nominated by a convention of which Reuther was an active member. The influence of organized labor in some sections of the Democratic party was never compared with the influence of the medical lobby (AMA) or organized big business (NAM) in the Republican Convention, but rather with the Bolshevik takeover in Russia in October 1917. Thus Walter Reuther, like his brother Victor an active Christian layman, who like his brother nearly lost his life fighting the Communist conspiracy long before various adventurers discovered that professional anti-communism was a way to make money, joined Bishop G. Bromley Oxnam, Dr. Martin Luther King, Jr., and Senator John F. Kennedy as a special target of the nativist element. Unfortunately, the prevailing rural and village background of most Protestant clergymen made them ready apologists for the Baals, the gods of production who still defy the God of righteousness and justice.

After the Civil War, the first surge of nativism died out for a time. When, in 1884, a Protestant bigot raised the slogan of "Rum, Romanism and Rebellion" against the Democratic party the reaction was so great that it cost the Republican candidate the election. Mr. James G. Blaine of Maine, who paid the price for the Rev. Dr. Burchard's malapropism, accepted defeat with these words:

> As the Lord sent upon us an ass in the shape of a preacher, and a rainstorm, to lessen our vote in New York, I am disposed to feel resigned to the dispensation of defeat, which flowed directly from these agencies.[10]

[10] Odegard, Peter H., ed., *Religion and Politics* (New Brunswick, N.J.: Rutgers University Press, 1960), pp. 36–40.

When, in 1928, Al Smith was candidate for the Democratic party, Protestant nativism again delivered substantial blocs of the vote to the Republican party. Admittedly, Al Smith was a personality who jarred old-line Protestant ideas at a number of points: he smoked big cigars and wore a brown derby, he talked with an East Side accent, he was avowedly "wet" at a time when leading officials were still verbally "dry" (although an honest attempt was no longer being made at national level to enforce Prohibition), and —he was a Roman Catholic. The most militant opposition to Smith was composed of organizations of "white, native-born Gentile citizens" united "to maintain forever white supremacy"; their program rang with such phrases as "pure Americanism," "mongrelization," "old stock American," "Nordic race," "alienism," and pointed to a climax with the statements,

> America was Protestant from birth.
> She must remain Protestant, if the Nordic stock is to finish its destiny. . . . Rome shall not rule us.[11]

The technical word for such ideological politics is *nativism,* and it is of the same political genus as Falangism, Peronisme, Fascism, and Nazism.

During the 1960 election, determined effort was again made to arouse the same prejudice against the candidacy of Senator John F. Kennedy that had worked so well against Governor Smith in 1928, and the most accurate survey shows that it cost him about four and a half million votes. Protestant nativism combined anti-Negro and anti-Semitic forces with those who hated labor, refugees, the UN, and foreign aid. "Know-Nothingism" became again a powerful force in predominantly Protestant areas.

Among the ignorant the forged "Oath of the Knights of Columbus" was circulated, frequently by use of the same mailing lists used earlier for distribution of the false "Protocols of the Elders of Zion." Prominent native fascists, including some who had been indicted for treason during the

11 Ibid., p. 45.

war with Hitler's Germany, came out of obscurity to join the new crusade. While a revived Ku Klux Klan and like organs of the Protestant underworld concentrated in rural towns and villages throughout the Deep South, semi-intellectual organs like Protestants and Other Americans United (POAU) appealed to the old-stock Americans of higher social and educational status. Saddest of all was the extent to which Protestant clergymen fell into the trap, discovering in anti-Catholicism a popularity and influence which they had not enjoyed for years. For Protestant Americans who had long since abandoned the disciplines and missionary effort which had once characterized the Methodists and Baptists and Disciples in winning the unchurched, could still be counted upon to remember they were—if nothing else—anti-Roman Catholic.

Among the religious bodies which took a public stand against election of a Roman Catholic were the following:

The Southern Baptist Convention (9,000,000 members);

The Assemblies of God Church, Springfield, Missouri (1,000,000 members);

The American Baptist Association (600,000 members);

The Conservative Baptist Association of America (275,-000 members);

The General Association of Regular Baptist Churches (126,000 members);

The Ministers of the Church of God, Cleveland, Tennessee (163,000 members);

The Augustana Lutheran Church (582,000 members);

The Pentecostal Freewill Baptist Conference, Inc. (20,-000 members).

Representatives of the Pentecostal Holiness Church and other smaller groups joined in the general attack. The National Association of Evangelicals became a focal center for the assault, and Reformation Sunday 1960 (October 30) was used as an occasion of assault on Senator John F. Kennedy's candidacy.

The traditional prestige structure of American religion can, in fact, be illustrated by the denominational preference of the American presidents. As might be expected, the Harvard wing of the New England standing order—Unitarianism—scored early and well with John Adams, John Quincy Adams, Millard Fillmore, and William Howard Taft. The Virginia tradition gave Anglicanism a head start, with George Washington, James Madison, and James Monroe; Thomas Jefferson, frequently claimed as a "freethinker," also paid his dues to the parish. Presidents who were Episcopalian after disestablishment were William Henry Harrison, John Tyler, Zachary Taylor, Franklin Pierce, Chester A. Arthur, and—perhaps the most ardent layman of them all—Franklin D. Roosevelt. Presbyterianism, powerful in the movement for independence and preeminent in educational leadership during the formative years of the Republic (1750–1850), can claim Andrew Jackson, James Buchanan, Grover Cleveland, Benjamin Harrison, Woodrow Wilson, and Dwight D. Eisenhower. These are the significant connections: Unitarians (4), Episcopalians (10), and Presbyterians (6). Other denominational preferences were scattered: Baptists (2), Congregationalists (1), Disciples (1—the only clergyman to be president), Quakers (1), Dutch Reformed (2). Abraham Lincoln, whose great presidential messages have never been equaled for orientation in the world and the mind of the Bible, belonged to no church. No Jew has ever been President, although several distinguished cabinet members and justices of the Supreme Court have been of that faith. The most significant break-through came in 1960, with the election of a Roman Catholic to the presidency.

Jewry Leaves the Ghetto

The creative thinking in the Jewish community is vigorous and suggestive to those who come from other traditions. The Jews, like the Roman Catholics, have had considerably less time than the Protestants to develop a view of the relation of religious society and civilization appropriate to the American setting. During the centuries of "Christendom" the ghetto was a logical counterpart, combining political and religious power in a similar way. For long, the leaders of the Jewish communities in the New World continued the ways learned in Christian Europe. As late as June 12, 1945, in dealing with teachings deemed heretical by the Orthodox, Orthodox rabbis voted a *herem*, a writ of excommunication, against an offending author. Then a young rabbi placed the offending book upon a table and attempted to burn it. The Rabbinical Assembly of America, the national organization of the Conservative rabbinate, stated in protest that they denied "the authority of an outside body to sit in judgment on one of our colleagues." This was indeed the reply appropriate to America's voluntaryism; but the Orthodox were at this moment still living in "Christendom" and its counterpart, the ghetto.[12]

At first, the process of Americanization showed itself in the development of English-language services like those of liberal Christian congregations. Many Jewish congregations[13] shifted to Sunday observance in place of the Sabbath. Jewish "Sunday Schools" emerged, and a Young Men's Hebrew Association and Young Women's Hebrew Association (Y.M.H.A. and Y.W.H.A.) arose parallel to the Y.M.C.A. and Y.W.C.A. In most respects the liberal Jewish belief and practice differed but little from those of the liberal Protestant congregations down the street. Rabbis as well as enlightened Jewish families celebrated Christmas with their "Christian" (i.e., Gentile) neighbors, since it has become a folk festival without specifically theological connotations—as more than one Jewish writer candidly observed.

[12] See "Thoughts About the Future of Christianity and Judaism: A Christian Views Reconstructionism," XIII *The Reconstructionist* (1947), 4:10.

[13] Judaism in America is divided into three sections: Orthodox, Conservative, and Reformed. Generally speaking, "congregation" is the term used by the Orthodox, "synagogue" is used by the Conservatives, and "temple" by the Reformed. The problem of general nomenclature is almost as difficult as with "church," "sect," "denomination," "cult," in Christian or semi-Christian circles. See Wach, Joachim, *Church, Denomination and Sect* (Evanston, Ill.: Seabury-Western Theological Seminary, 1946).

Although the majority of Jews remained observant, these were not the people with active intercourse with the Gentile community. It seemed to the languid that American Jews, too, were well on their way to assimilation into the American, non-sectarian religion. Always important in intellectual and cultural affairs when given the opportunity, Jews contributed mightily to the rise of a simple humanism and also the various *avant-garde* movements of the depression years of the 1930s. There are still evidences of this Unitarian style of religion, but the tide has changed. More than anything else it was the Zionist cause, its logic powerfully supported by the madness of Hitler's pogroms, that stayed the secularization of Judaism and produced in America a renaissance of Jewish religious thought.

The first impulses toward a renewed emphasis upon Hebrew study, community life, and cultivation, came from the drive for the re-establishment of a Jewish state in the Near East. Great Americans, of whom Louis D. Brandeis was perhaps the best known, supported the Zionist cause for years before assimilation ceased to be the primary goal of Americanized Jews. But with the rise of Hitler, the founding of a Jewish state in Palestine became a real issue to American Jewry. In spite of the efforts of successive British governments to sabotage the pledge made with the Balfour Declaration of November 1, 1917, American Jewry lined up almost solidly in support of the movement of refugees from Nazism into the mandated area. In spite of universal sympathy for Britain's courageous and sacrificial stand against Nazi imperialism, a stand in which Jewish volunteers played their part, the plight of those who had escaped the gas chambers and were stranded in postwar Europe was too desperate to admit delay: American Jews and many Christian leaders joined in support of measures, sometimes "illegal," to implement the movement of Jews into Palestine.

Although after the founding of the new state of Israel considerable financial support has come to it from the restitution policies of the German Federal Republic, the main base of assistance remains American Jewry. Bond issues are sold in annual campaigns in the U.S.A., and American goodwill has helped to protect Israel from the constant threat of invasion by the Arab League governments on her borders. Hitler destroyed European Jewry but he brought a renaissance of religious and cultural self-consciousness to American Jews. Today American Jewry numbers more than half of the world's Jewish population, and the Jewish communities here are the center of financial and cultural strength among those of that faith.

The new vision of Judaism in the American setting has been termed "Catholic Israel" by Solomon Schechter. His term would have been inappropriate for a Judaism which was conceived as a mere transfer of ghetto practice to the New World. But it is appropriate for a Judaism which has accepted the status of Judaism in America for what it is: a matter of voluntary affiliation. Even though the ghetto complex, after hundreds of years of Gentile pressure and persecution, is harder for the Jews to cast aside, the process is already well advanced through which Jews as well as Catholics and Protestants can affiliate or disaffiliate at will.

When all is said and done, this is a far happier situation than under the style of political and cultural coercion which so long governed the misuse of religion to support and accomplish tribal or national purposes. In it we see the emergence of a genuine basis for religious universalism, for religion which is identifiable by faith and witness rather than by accident of birth or citizenship.

"Post-Protestant" America

Perhaps the most significant positive developments in the present religious scene in America are the rise of "unitive Protestantism" (Professor John T. McNeill's phrase) and the emergence of the dialogue involving Protestants, Catholics, and Jews. In both of these frontier situations the most serious impediment has been the lack of clarity in Protestant circles as to the nature of the Protestant witness. The great churches of the nineteenth-century expansion have remained proudly non-theological, when not actively anti-intellectual. Some of their spokesmen have openly opposed the articulation of a doctrine of the church. The judgment expressed on Congregationalism in an editorial in *The Christian Century* during the struggles of that association to achieve a base of union with the Evangelical and Reformed Church might apply equally well to several other denominations which had identified themselves with the old image of "Christian America."

> The stature which this denomination has lost in recent years was lost mainly because too much had been taken for granted for too long. It was assumed that a denomination which had contributed so much to American culture knew its own mind, understood its own genius, was inwardly united.[14]

During the generations when the old-line Protestant churches were at peace with the carefully cultivated image of "Christian America" (i.e., Protestant America), there was little necessity for theological clarity. In "post-Protestant America," however, the Protestant churches are forced to make a real effort at self-understanding. This effort is the burden of the hour. There is the way of protectionism and vindictiveness, the way of reaction and romantization of the past. This is the way of Protestant nativism, of unwillingness to face the fact that at the beginning of the nineteenth century the U.S.A., officially Protestant, was in fact a heathen nation. There is another way: the way of the open face of truth; of full, free, and informed discussion with fellow citizens who presently have other convictions; of faith in the Lord who rules the future. The latter is the way of positive witness rather than anxiety and resentment.

In 1800 the challenge before the Protestant churches was to win the people back into the churches. In the 1960s the challenge is to introduce the kind of instruction which will serve to make meaningful the tremendous memberships which have been won. This is the way of self-understanding which can make a true dialogue possible.

[14] LXXIII *The Christian Century* (1956), 26:767.

Even though the churches which had the most rapid expansion have remained fixed in statistical concerns, there is ample evidence that the period of sensational accessions has come to an end. In the 1961 *Yearbook of the American Churches* there is very clear evidence that confusion as to the Protestant image in the minds of church members and other Americans is beginning to have fateful consequences in growth of membership as well as in church discipline and in civic affairs. Catholic membership has steadily grown over recent years, although not as rapidly as before the end of the great immigrations. Now the growth in either confession must be made primarily from the unchurched of the population, and by family growth, rather than from any newly arrived from Europe. In these years Catholicism is forging ahead. While the population increased 1.8 per cent during 1960, Roman Catholic membership rose to 40,871,-302 (a gain of 1,361,794 or 3.4 per cent); Protestant membership reached 62,543,502 (a gain of 1.7 per cent). Of the total population, 33.8 per cent are Protestants and 23.1 per cent are Catholics. Another 10 per cent may be estimated for Jewish membership and that of religions not reporting or not included in the three major faith groupings. In sum, two thirds of Americans are listed now on the rolls of organized religious bodies. This is the largest voluntary membership in the history of any part of Western civilization.

More than that, polls have shown that 96 per cent of the American people consider themselves members of churches. Fully one third of those who say, "I'm a Methodist," or "I'm a Baptist," or "I'm a Presbyterian," and so on do not in fact appear on any church rolls. In contrast with "post-Christian" Europe, where as high as one third of those on the church rolls may actually be anti-clerical or even vote Communist in elections, in America the unidentified are pro-religious.

From the above, several very important conclusions can be drawn:

1. Americans are, comparatively speaking, very religious in a general sort of way;

2. one out of three has denominational preference or prejudice, but gives it no positive expression;

3. the Roman Catholic Church is the church body most successful in capitalizing on this inarticulate "spirituality," although from time to time negative campaigns of Protestant nativism may slow the movement to Rome;

4. there is little evidence of a strong and positive evangelicalism which would serve to accredit the Gospel according to the Protestant principle.

The American Religion: A Popular Heresy

Integral parts of "the American way of life" are ". . . instant coffee, homogenized milk, TV, hamburgers, and church."[15] Many churches join without hesitation in the billboard and newspaper slogan, "Go to the Church of Your Choice, but GO TO CHURCH!" Politicians regularly proclaim Christianity to be the bulwark of private property and the guard against communism. When occasional prophetic spirits protest that the Church has another primary purpose, both antecedent and subsequent to the United States, they are publicly attacked as "soft on Communism." Numerous religious adventurers, supporting their own "private enterprise" by (tax-exempt) frauds with such names as "Christian Mobilization," "the American Federation of Churches," "Protestant Economics, Inc.," and so on, do not hesitate to enlist the support of the ignorant and fearful by slanderous attacks on the ecumenical movement and the acknowledged leaders of the Christian churches.[16]

More dangerous, perhaps, is the way in which various "interfaith chapels" are springing up in various public institutions and centers, expressing a vague harmonism of all religion. These are not founded on a clear-headed and open dialogue. Rather their foundation is the same "non-sectarian religion," or "confessionless Christianity," or "spirituality"

[15] Wilson, Sloan, *The Man in the Grey Flannel Suit* (New York: Simon & Schuster, 1955), p. 73.

[16] Roy, Ralph Lord, *Apostles of Discord* (Boston: Beacon Press, 1953).

that played such a significant role in Nazi party strategy against the Catholic and Evangelical churches of Germany, and is presently cultivated by various "positive" and "progressive" religious movements in Poland, Hungary, and other Communist satellites. If "the American religion" continues to emerge, bringing with it the hearty and uncritical affirmation of everything American, the time may yet come when believing Jews, Catholics, and Protestants will have to face up to tribal religion in its more demonic form. In that day they will learn, as has been learned by the religious remnants who have remained faithful in the face of other totalitarianism, that they have much in common besides a goodly land.

Protestant "Moralism"

Reinhold Niebuhr (b. 1892) has done more than any other Protestant theologian to point out the weaknesses of verbalism divorced from witness, of "moralism," in the American churches. According to the view he usually expresses, many of the American religious bodies derive from movements which Ernst Troeltsch identified as "sectarian" or "sect-type," and they are constantly attempting to apply simplicistic solutions to problems of political and social ethics of which they have no real grasp. The "church type" has a more subtle approach, however, and is not so naive as to suggest that the problems of natural law and order can be solved if only politicians would avoid "power politics" and practice the Sermon on the Mount. That Protestant "moralism" has been, and continues to be, offensive and exasperating scarcely needs discussion. But it does not really come alone from those groups which fit most perfectly Troeltsch's typology. "Moralism," as a public stance of American Protestant churches, is primarily the attitude of religious bodies which have come to think of themselves as the religious voice of a society when in fact they are in the minority. Not "sectarianism" but "culture-religion" is the key word.

When Methodist or Baptist churches—for example—pass

pious resolutions on public issues, resolutions which have no binding authority on their own members and no real influence in public life, they are guilty of that self-righteousness of tone and presumptuousness of judgment which Professor Niebuhr condemns as "sectarian," "perfectionist," and "moralistic." If they were really of the "sect-type," however, the pronouncements would reflect a disciplined minority witness. Actually, as in the anti-saloon and anti-evolution campaigns, such churches are asking legislation to control that thought or action among all citizens which they cannot control among their own members. They are assuming the stance of spokesmen for the religious mind of Georgia or Texas or Iowa. They are, in short, disclosing the mind-set of once dominant Protestant bodies grown accustomed to speaking for the majority and continuing to talk the same way after they have ceased to have the constituents or the moral authority so to do. The society has become pluralistic: the Jews and the Catholics are there, and other Protestant bodies. Their own members no longer follow with discipline: statistical success has been bought at the price of lowered entrance and membership standards.

The once dominant groups may continue to name the chaplains in state institutions, to open the football games and state legislatures' sessions with prayer, and in virtual alliance with the Republican party try to defeat Jewish and Catholic candidates. They cannot, however, except in a negative sense, affect public policy very profoundly. Their words no longer carry authority, within their own constituencies or without. Their "style" is not that of the "sect" leader, who tells the princes of Moravia that if "all men were as we are there would be no occasion for wars" (Jakob Huter). Their style is that of a corrupt and decaying establishment—of a Protestantism once dominant by tradition and by zeal, which is trying to stay so by presumption and jealously guarded privilege. "Moralism" is the tone of voice of a religious body which has stood still in its thinking while a society shifts from monochromatic to polychromatic religious pattern. It is the tone of voice of resolutions which once had authority and are now empty of significance.

The Recovery of the Tragic Note

The note of tragedy for which Niebuhr is justly famous re-entered American theology when some men became aware of the implications of the rise of totalitarianism in Europe. The true significance of the Nazi and Communist pseudo-religions has not yet penetrated the hinterland, and many American church leaders simply brush "European pessimism" aside and stalwartly reaffirm the happy harmonism of the nineteenth century. In the most live theological circles in America, however, there is growing up the realization that the nineteenth century is at an end, and that it ended with the rise of the most terrible apostasy and mass defections experienced by Christendom since Islam swept through and captured the ancient strongholds of Christianity in North Africa. Totalitarianism arose not in Africa, Asia, North America, or the islands of the sea—where Christianity was spreading most rapidly; it appeared in the shadow of St. Peter's, in the heartland of the Reformation, in Moscow (the "third Rome" of Eastern Orthodoxy). This was the tragedy of Christendom, that in her decline she spawned the most monstrous ideologies and political religions. Today the most sensitive younger theologians of Europe speak of their time as a "post-Christian era."

The warning that comes to America, that is declared to her by her ablest theologians, is that "Christendom" is no longer a viable concept, that the nineteenth-century continuum has split apart. Nevertheless, it is a serious error—though a common one—to bracket the churches in America and the churches of Europe in a common destiny. True, the most serious challenge confronting the faith in America is also tribal religion, Protestant nativism, apostasy of the sort that many of the churches in Europe also have had to struggle with. The words of Professor Edmund Schlink on the condition of religion in pre-Hitler Germany might be transferred without amendment or alteration to popular religion of the present in America:

. . . people had grown accustomed to regard God primarily as the protector of ordered family life, a help in the education of children and a friend in the events of life such as leaving school, marriage and death. He had become the guarantor of national and civic security, in the midst of the insecurities of this world.[17]

But the churches in Europe have lived through the recent eclipse of "Christendom," whereas that system ended in America with the collapse of the colonial state churches. Only the myth remains to haunt us and bedevil our deliberations. There remains in fact but the choice between a romantic and reactionary myth of Protestant America and on the other hand a joyful acceptance of our rightful place among the Younger Churches of a century and a half of triumphant missions.

The Rediscovery of the Dialogue

Our profile ends with "the dialogue," for it is here that the trial of strength between nativism and evangelical faith comes into focus. Just as the great test of moral discipline comes in the elimination of racial discrimination, so the great test of spiritual discipline comes in the encounter of persons from the three great faiths: Catholicism, Protestantism, Judaism. Neither the moral nor the theological test has yet been passed by American Protestantism, and it is the same elements which are holding back at both points. The situation is strikingly like that which the European churches confronted in dealing with the tribal religion of Nazism. Theologically and ecclesiologically those who are determined that the American churches shall bless "our way of life" stand exactly where the collaborators with the Nazis, the "German Christians," stood twenty-five years ago. Theirs is the same curious mixture of creedless "spirituality," of treason toward the universal church.

[17] Schlink, Edmund, "The Witness of the German Church Struggle," in *The Universal Church in God's Design* (London: SCM Press, 1948), p. 99.

To clarify the situation, and to promise triumph over the present impasse, however, these positive factors can be found in the "post-Protestant era" in America:

1. our Protestant churches are at the crest of a century and a half of home missions, not at the latter end of a corroded establishment;

2. our problems in the Protestant churches, as acute as they are theologically and ethically and morally, are the problems of "new Christians," not the problems of disenchanted and discouraged nominal Christians;

3. the missionary impulse, and the active "world-mindedness" related to it, remain a vital constitutive element in all of our churches;

4. there are powerful Catholic and Jewish communities of faith in the Republic to give the lie to nativism and—now emerging from their ghettos—to engage with Protestants in a vigorous discussion of the nature of a just social order and a righteous commonwealth.

For all of these things we must give thanks and take heart in the future. Anxiety, longing for a lost past (imaginary), fear of the future, are simply signs of faithlessness.

The author has not disguised his point of view, but rather presented it frankly in the hope that his argument will be met with the same candor and readiness to discuss that he has tried to show on his part. The discipline of historical reflection is the conduct of "the dialogue with the past." The situation of religious voluntaryism and pluralism in which the American Protestants now find themselves, understood historically, is a positive good—both theologically and politically. As an evangelical Christian, the author expects less trouble from Roman Catholics and Jews than from fellow Protestants in presenting this introduction to American church history. For the Protestants, accustomed for long generations to operate from a position of prestige and preeminence, have not as yet accepted the religious situation in the U.S.A. for what it is: post-Protestant. Neither have they yet accepted the religious situation at the beginning of the Republic for what it was: heathen. Therefore they are not yet able to capitalize on the great potential of a situation in which their view of the faith is in open competition with the alternatives.

The Protestants need to learn to think of themselves as "Younger Churches" in a mission field; they still think of themselves as part of north European Christendom—"Protestant America" as it was before formal disestablishment, before the generations of mass evangelism, before the great immigrations of Catholic, Jewish, and Eastern Orthodox millions. The future of Protestantism in the U.S.A. rests quite literally with the outcome of a decision to be faced in this generation: a choice between retreat to Protestant culture-religion, increasingly pressed into retirement from public life and finally to end as a ghetto, and the alternative —a new and joyous break-through of evangelical faith sustaining a disciplined witness.

The worst enemy of the evangelical understanding of the Gospel in the U.S.A.—far more serious an adversary than Catholicism or Judaism, far more heretical than any of the cults or prophetic movements like Christian Science or Mormonism or Jehovah's Witnesses—is Protestant nativism. The sin and error of this phenomenon is not propositional: it is a matter of timing. Those who dream of the "good old days" of Protestant hegemony do not trust the providence of God. The problem of the nativists is not "spirituality."

After all, meetings of the Klan and of White Citizens Councils characteristically start with prayer.[18]

Their problem is that they have lost sight of the Lord of History, the Lord who guided their fathers in their time of trial and who might be called upon again if their children were less anxious, less embittered, less frustrated by apparent loss of status.

In a dramatic ceremony during National Brotherhood Week, February 1961, the non-fiction award of the year was granted to a book entitled *An American Dialogue*.

[18] Shinn, Roger, "The Lordship of Christ—and American Society," XX *Encounter* (1959), 4:462.

This book, written in collaboration between a brilliant Protestant theologian (Robert McAfee Brown) and a distinguished Catholic theologian (Gustave Weigel), with an introduction by one of the greatest contemporary Jewish scholars (Will Herberg), marked the high point to date of an expanding network of discussions between representatives of the three major faiths in the Republic. These discussions, sometimes spontaneously emerging on a local basis and sometimes fostered by national movements like the National Conference of Christians and Jews and the Association for the Co-ordination of University Religious Affairs, call for a maturity and self-understanding which all three faith groups have yet to gain in a setting of voluntaryism and pluralism.

And "the dialogue," as important as it is for right relations between fellow citizens, may very well have its ultimate value in helping faithful men and women of the three traditions to overcome the fears and protectionist practices of centuries of persecution and hatred, and to discover again what a good thing it is for brethren to dwell in peace together. The Protestantism, Catholicism, and Judaism which is shaped in part by the dialogue will become better than any of them was before—either in the "good old days" of the Founding Fathers, or in the good old times of the religious wars of Europe. It may even come to pass that the God whose purposes brood over the future will point out to our children or children's children some better way than the well-worn paths of denominational separation and suspicion which their fathers knew so well.

INDEX